Easy*Riders*

EasyRiders
Cruising the Long White Cloud

PAUL AND VAL DAVIS

HarperCollins*Publishers* (New Zealand) Limited

First published 2000
HarperCollins*Publishers (New Zealand) Limited*
P.O. Box 1, Auckland

Copyright © Paul and Val Davis 2000

Photographs copyright © Paul Davis 2000,
except page 41, copyright © Alan Whitt

Paul and Val Davis assert the moral right to be
identified as the authors of this work.

All rights reserved. No part of this publication may
be reproduced, stored in a retrieval system or
transmitted in any form or by any means, electronic,
mechanical, photocopying, recording or otherwise,
without the prior written permission of the
publishers.

ISBN 1 86950 357 0
Designed by Jan Harris
Typeset by Pauline Whimp
Printed by Brebner Print, Auckland

Introduction

Easy Riders is not your average motorcycle book. Certainly, these pages contain photographs of some quite outstanding bikes, and some unique, hand built machines. But it is the people who own these bikes who are the real focus of this book. Their shared passion — their obsession, if you like — is motorcycles, and their stories — told wherever possible in their own words — offer an insight into what makes them tick both as motorcyclists and as New Zealanders.

We, on the other hand, are not motorcyclists. However, one day, sitting at a T-junction, waiting to turn right onto what was then State Highway 1, we watched a couple of motorcycles go past. And then a few more. And perhaps another dozen. We started counting. Ten, twenty, forty, fifty. We lost count at just over two hundred. Just when we thought we might stand a chance of pulling out onto the road, along came a little red Vespa, manfully chugging along behind the big boys . . . only it turned out that the Vespa was probably ridden by a lovely lady called Peggy, and not by a man at all. 'Probably', because it was only after we started researching the stories of the people who appear in this book that we met Peggy and found out about her passion for Vespas, and red ones in particular. Naturally, she couldn't be certain it was her we saw that day, but it could well have been. If not, it was someone very like her. Regardless of the rider, the sight of that little red Vespa following all those motorcycles had us in stitches. But it also provided the spark of inspiration that was the genesis of this book.

Researching, photographing and writing *Easy Riders* has been a lengthy, though pleasurable process. We are very grateful to all the wonderful people who agreed to appear in the book. Many of them travelled a considerable distance to reach our studio for the photographic session and subsequent interrogation. Without exception, we enjoyed meeting and getting to know each and every one of them. Thanks are due, too, to Sue and Ian at HarperCollins, for their patience and forbearance.

Obviously there are many other folk out there with a tale to tell, people who are equally passionate about motorcycles. Please forgive us for not finding you. And do contact us in case we manage to produce a second volume of *Easy Riders*. In the meantime, we hope you enjoy *this* book.

Val and Paul Davis

Reg Woods

When I got my first Honda Gold Wing it was love at first sight

'Fantasy' is the name proud owner Reg Woods has had airbrushed onto his Honda Gold Wing Trike — along with space ships, asteroids, a galaxy or two and a cosmonaut! As well as being a biker, Reg is also an avid Star Trek enthusiast and a man who likes to 'live' his dreams. Now in his mid-60s, Reg's passion for motorcycles continues unabated, only now he prefers the three-wheeled kind.

'I damaged my knee when I tried microlighting. I crashed on landing . . . I was evidently not meant to be an angel! Lifting my rather large and heavy bike up onto the centre stand was painful, so after some discussion with the wife I converted the bike into a trike.'

Reg had the trike conversion kit sent over from the United States and, with the help of a good friend, his two-wheeler was transformed into a three wheeler.

'I've ridden motorcycles on and off since I was sixteen years of age. When I got my first Honda Gold Wing — a 1976 model — it was love at first sight. With some reservations and conditions, my wife finally agreed to letting me buy my heart's desire. She never dreamed where this fixation would lead. Over the years I have restored and updated several Gold Wings, increasing the cc ratings as I've gone along.'

Belonging to several motorcycle clubs, Reg and Fantasy have travelled all roads from Cape Reinga to Stewart Island. Together they have taken part in rallies, charity rides, school galas and fundraising events — and Reg has a badge from each event to prove it. It came as no surprise to learn that cuddly Reg also puts on his Santa outfit once a year and brings smiles to lots of children's faces.

'Being of a somewhat rotund physique with white hair and a beard does help,' says Reg.

1988 Honda Gold Wing
1500cc
6 cylinder

Russell Hardman

We have some really awesome roads in New Zealand

Russell and his wife, Yvonne, are a farming couple from Waimate in the South Island. In common with so many of the motorcycling enthusiasts we met on our travels, Russell had to put family commitments ahead of his dreams for quite some years. Nowadays, however, he is free to indulge his passion and Yvonne, now equally enthusiastic, rides with him.

'Yvonne had never been on the back of a motorcycle, but had put up with me always wanting one. The day came when we decided we were in a position to look at getting a bike and I found an old CB900, which Yvonne absolutely loved. We bought the bike and after a few practice runs we not only went to the 1999 Glenorchy rally on it but we also did a tour of the South Island. Great! In just over a month we managed to clock up five thousand kilometres. We already had a trip up north planned so we decided something a little more modern was in order. It was then that we purchased our first Kawasaki ZZR1100.

'This bike fulfilled our needs almost perfectly. It was comfortable to ride and yet still performed extremely well. It took us on club rides and to rallies, as well as touring up north twice. In just on twelve months we travelled twenty-two thousand kilometres. At this point, with ninety-nine thousand kilometres on the clock, we thought it might be a good idea to purchase a new bike and, as the old ZZR had worked so well for us, there was no need to change models, only years.

'I'm often asked why I like bikes. It's a hard question to answer and those who ride all have different reasons for riding. I ride because I love the feeling of having all that power at my finger tips. I ride because I love the feeling you get knowing that your life depends on that two inches of rubber that keeps you on the tarseal. I ride because we have some really awesome roads in New Zealand, and I'm not talking about the big, long straights we have in Canterbury — they're boring. I love the east coast of the North Island, but my favourite road would have to be the one from Culverden through to Nelson, over the Lewis Pass.

'Both Yvonne and myself love to attend rallies and to catch up with the other bikers there. The ride to a rally is usually a good one, too, and there's always a good party.'

Kawasaki ZZR1100

Max. horsepower: 108 km (147 PS) at 10,500 rpm

Max. torque: 110 N-m at 8500 rpm

Turning radius: 3 metres

Overall length: 2165 mm

Overall width: 730 mm

Overall height: 1205 mm

Wheelbase: 1500 mm

Road clearance: 110 mm

Dry weight: 233 kg

Engine type: DOHC, 16-valve 4-cylinder, 4-stroke, liquid cooled

Bore and stroke: 76 x 58 mm

Compression ratio: 11.0 : 1

Starter: electric

Carburettors: Keihin CVKD 40 x 4

Ignition system: Battery and coil (transistorised)

Transmission type: 6-speed, constant mesh, return shift

Chris Hyland

Fast, powerful and handles like a dream

'I have been fascinated by motorcycles since I was twelve years old when I built my first bike from a motor scooter engine and a home-made frame. The rest of my teenage years were dominated by motorcycles. Even my after-school job and first full time job were at a motorcycle shop. In my late teens, I began selling my collection of bikes. What with girlfriends who didn't like bikes and overseas travel, motorcycles seemed less important at the time.

'It was another twenty years before I owned a bike again. Maybe it was the prospect of turning forty, or just the desire to have some more fun that prompted me to start looking for a motorcycle. A friend had just bought a 1969 BSA, and he encouraged me to look for a classic bike. The idea appealed to me, as new bikes had changed so much from those I had known. It didn't take long for me to find a 1967 Triumph Bonneville. When I turned up at home on it, my wife thought I had gone mad!

'In 1967, the Bonneville was Triumph's top-of-the-line sports bike, and if you owned one, you had arrived. My Bonneville spent its early years in the United States, and came to New Zealand in 1981. The old Bonneville is a joy to ride and it is the ideal bike for a sunny Sunday afternoon cruise around the city. I will never sell the Bonneville as it is such a great piece of history and fun to own.

'In 1999 Triumph released the Sprint ST — and I just had to have one. It is fast, powerful and handles like a dream, allowing me to enjoy every kilometre of the great motorcycling roads we have in New Zealand. My wife could not understand my excitement and anticipation during the month-long wait between ordering and picking up the new Triumph Sprint. I picked up the bike on a sunny winter's day and rode to Tauranga and Rotorua, getting back to Auckland by five in the afternoon. It was a fantastic day.

'Motorcycling has not yet caught my wife's imagination, but when the sun is really warm and there are absolutely no grey clouds in sight I can tempt her with a ride around the waterfront for a coffee at Saint Heliers. Her confidence in motorcycling did not get off to a positive start — our first trip together on the Bonneville included a minor collision between my front wheel and the rear bumper of a car which stopped more quickly than I did. Fortunately, the only thing damaged was my ego and Teresa still hops on the back on those really sunny days.

'I'm currently restoring a 1968 Bonneville. It's in a million pieces now but this time next year it will be as good as new, and ready for a sunny Sunday afternoon.'

1967 Triumph Bonneville T120 R

650cc air-cooled parallel twin cylinder

Twin Amal carburettors and coil ignition

47 bhp at 6700 rpm

4-speed gearbox

Weight: 165 kg

1999 Triumph Sprint ST

955cc liquid-cooled in-line 3 cylinder

Multipoint sequential electronic fuel injection

Digital inductive electronic ignition

118 bhp at 9200 rpm

6-speed gearbox

Weight: 207 kg

Ken Campbell

The frame took about seven months to build

Ken Campbell has lived in the Matakana area north of Auckland all his life. His dad owned the local garage and Ken learned his engineering skills from a very early age.

'Dad taught me to weld when I was seven. He handed me a broken sewing needle, a really tiny thing and said, "There you are, son, try mending that." It took me a while to figure out how to do it, but I managed it. I don't know who was more surprised — Dad or me.

'I used to love mini-bikes and I made a few of my own. One day I tried to jump a pile of metal and I fell off. The exhaust pipe went into the top of my leg — even at the tender age of seven I was worried about my virility! It didn't stop me wanting to ride motorcycles, though, as you can see from this place.'

Whilst chatting to Ken it was indeed difficult not to be impressed by his amazing collection of vintage motorcycles and motorcycle parts, all neatly organised and displayed in his barn. Self-employed, Ken earns his living by repairing and restoring old motorcycles. He is often presented with a pile of rusty old parts, representing only about 20 per cent of an original motorcycle. He then sets about 'making' the remainder of the bike, thus restoring it to its former glory. Most of the restoration work is on pre-World War Two models. Ken admitted to spending most of his time in the barn, even when he is not officially 'working'. In Ken's case, the line between work and leisure is very blurred.

The barn sits adjacent to Ken's house — a house with a difference, designed and built by Ken himself. Remember the story of the three little pigs? The walls of Ken's environmentally friendly home are constructed from bales of straw, plastered on both sides. With an engineer's attention to detail, the beautiful home boasts a wealth of design features and is a credit to Ken's ingenuity and skill.

In the foreground of the photograph is Ken's pride and joy, a replica 1912 Indian 8-valve Board Track Racer, which Ken has painstakingly built entirely from scratch. This is Ken's own bike, a real labour of love.

'The frame took about seven months to build in my spare time. I planned to race the bike, and three months before race day I made the engine. I was going to use a standard road engine but changed my mind. In the end, I decided to go all the way and make an eight-valver. I'm glad I did. On race day I didn't win, but I did manage to pull two second places and I was really pleased with the bike. I built it to be as near perfect in every detail as I could.'

Replica 1912 Indian Board Track Racer

8 valve

1000cc V-Twin

Bill & Anne Reed

For all motorcyclists who enjoy a bit on the side

As founder members of the Sidecar Owners Register, Bill and Ann have an enduring passion for motorcycles and sidecars. After thirty-five years of marriage to Bill — and his bike — Ann has no regrets . . .

'Bill and I are not just married to each other, we are married to motorcycles. I'm sure it was written in the contract. I started learning to ride motorcycles thirty years ago, only to find that I was no good on two wheels. "Try three," said Bill. Perfect. I didn't fall off. I have been attached ever since, almost delivering our second son in the sidecar. Believe me, in a sidecar there is no room for dramas.

'In 1982 we placed an advertisement for "all motorcyclists who enjoy a bit on the side" to attend a rally at Waitomo. The response was overwhelming. Fifty-five outfits and trikes were there that first year. The following year there were seventy-five. The rallies continue on a national level and local gatherings provide fairly regular contact for members of the Sidecar Owners Register. We think of them all as extended family.'

Bill's father first introduced him to motorcycles in 1947, and his passion for bikes endures to this day. In 1998 Bill had a triple bypass heart operation. Within a matter of a few weeks he was up and on his way to attend the National Sidecar Rally in Otaki. When asked if he went on his bike, he replied, 'How else?'

Affectionately known as 'The Godfather' to other club members, here's Bill chatting about the early days . . .

'My dad owned a Norton Big Four outfit. One day Dad and I were stopped by the police. I was driving, Dad was in the sidecar. The policeman said, "How old are you, son?" It was with a sense of pride and achievement that I replied, "Twelve, sir."

'During the years since then I have had love-hate relationships with a variety of British machines. To the knowledgeable this means that I have slept with some and kicked others. Four years in the Merchant Navy enabled me to travel the world and experience riding in both friendly and hostile environments. By "friendly" I mean a country where you can legally blat around at whatever speed seems to be appropriate at the time. By "hostile" I mean somewhere where there is no law and the tracks and trails harbour life-threatening hazards unknown in New Zealand.

'I met Ann in 1962 whilst on leave and we married in 1965. Motorcycles are our preferred method of travel and a motorcycle and sidecar is the ultimate family machine. Needless to say I no longer sleep with my bike and with the advent of reliable machinery I no longer kick it either.

'All in all, I think that *now* is the best time to be a motorcyclist and *here* is the best place to be one.'

1987 Suzuki GS1100 G

Shaft drive

Bill made the leading link forks

Mark II Sabiston sidecar

Kevin Knight

When we go on runs, we like to go in style

'**My partner, Sue, shares my passion** for riding motorbikes; we own a 1500 Honda Gold Wing and trailer known as "Sweet As" and "Sweet As II". We are both members of the Ulysses Motorcycle Club. When we go on runs we like to go in style — the trailer filled with a twelve by nine foot tent with awning and airbeds, a gas cooker, a table and chairs — and I mustn't forget to mention the chilly bin full of ice for the whiskies! I average about forty miles per gallon and around thirty-five when towing the trailer. We love getting out on the open road and cruising the highways of both the North and South Islands of New Zealand. We have been on many organized rallies including the Brass Monkey (South Island) and the Cold Kiwi (North Island) and get a real buzz out of meeting other bikers with the same interests but from different walks of life.

'Doing charity runs and raising funds for the underprivileged gives us a real good feeling. I think these events are not promoted enough by the media.

'I have ridden for some twenty-five years now, both to work and for recreation, and I have found the Gold Wing to be a most reliable bike. She comes with a number of creature comforts, including a four-speaker stereo tape deck, cruise control, intercoms, reverse gear and loads of other accessories. The trailer adds a new dimension for camping. A bit different from when I first started with just the bare essentials! If and when I can't ride any more I intend to convert the Wing into a trike — the conversion kit can be imported from the United States.

'Riding on the open road tends to give you a different outlook on life — the sense of freedom you feel with the wind blowing by or the sun beaming down. I'd better not forget to mention the rain that sometimes buckets down as well, making the road as slippery as hell. The sudden gusts of wind certainly don't help, but that's all part of the joy of riding. One year, coming back from the Brass Monkey, I had sun, wind, rain, snow and whatever else could be thrown at me. At the end of a long ride there is a sense of accomplishment and a buzz that feels great, even when you're really tired. Other people who ride will know that feeling well and understand what I'm talking about. Then, of course, reality kicks in and it's back to the normal humdrum of life . . . so we can start saving up to do it all over again.'

1989 1500 K Honda Gold Wing

Engine size : 1520 k

Engine type: OHC, opposed six, liquid-cooled

Fuel capacity: 6.3 gallons

Starting system: electric

Transmission: 5-speed

Final drive: shaft

Chassis: steel dual shock

Wheel base: 66.9 inches

Seat height: 30.3 inches

Dry weight: 795.8 lb

Marg & Pete Boland

I do all my own machining, painting and mechanical work

Pete Boland has been a motorcycle fanatic as long as he can remember. His wife, Marg, now the proud owner of a 750 Suzuki Intruder, was for many years decidedly less than enthusiastic. Her first experience on a motorcycle may well explain why! Pete tells the story . . .

'I've always been into motorbikes and when I got married I think Marg hoped it would be a passing phase. Initially she accepted it and even occasionally rode pillion. That was, until I took her for a ride on my 750 Triple Kawasaki — the first time the front wheel gently elevated skyward Marg insisted I went directly home. She didn't get on another bike for over ten years!

'When I joined the Ulysses Club Marg would occasionally come on runs on pillion. It didn't half cramp my style — I was scared of repeating my earlier mistake. Then, one New Year's Eve six years ago, she made the mistake of mentioning to a friend that she might sit her bike licence on my son's TS185. The next day, Marg and my youngest son left for a seven-day tramp around Mount Ruapehu. On her return — and much to her amazement — I showed Marg her new motorbike, a Honda VT250. Marg duly sat her licence and hasn't looked back since.

'Bikes are in my blood and I enjoy working on them almost as much as riding them, so being able to share this with Marg is a very special thing.

'Bikers are a resourceful bunch and we have learned to repair our machines on the side of the road using materials that are to hand and the sparsest of tool kits. Many a time a bike has limped home with parts wired together or held on with duct tape. I remember one occasion when my bike decided to throw its chain. I walked about a mile back up the road and found the broken chain, but close inspection revealed that the crankcase had been holed. I hunted around and found an aluminium label off some fencing wire. I laid the bike on its side, first removing the petrol tank so that the oil was well away from where the hole was. Wetting my hankie with petrol, I cleaned the area around the hole. Using the handle of a screwdriver I then moulded the label to fit over the hole. Using the blade of the screwdriver I made two holes to line up with the crankcase bolts. Finally, having smeared the label with RTV, I removed the crankcase screws and screwed them home through the label, thus sealing the hole. After replacing the chain, adding a new joining link, we were back under way. This repair lasted for a number of months with no leaks until I got time to repair it properly.'

Bikes in photograph are from left to right:

Kawasaki H2 750
750cc
3 cylinder
2-stroke

Kawasaki Z1b1000
1000cc
4 cylinder

Suzuki VS750 Intruder
750cc
V-twin engine
Water-cooled

Honda CBX1000
1000cc
6 cylinder
24 valves

Kawasaki ZX-10
1000cc
4 cylinder
Water-cooled
150 BHP

Ross Pennell

Once you have motorcycling in your blood it is there forever

Ross — better known as Rosco — Pennell has had a lasting love affair with Harley-Davidson motorcycles. As he says, 'They build other bikes to fall off and Harleys to ride.' He's not at all biased, of course, it's just that for Rosco there is no other type of motorcycle. He started out, however, on a humbler machine:

'About 1962 this young fella Rosco needed to get mobile. I had just started work, so had no money, but when my eyes fell upon this old, beat-up 1948 MAC Velocette and the guy only wanted ninety quid for it and he would finance it for me... well, yes, then I became a biker (much to my mother's displeasure). That motorcycle kept me as fit as a fiddle as I had to push start it every morning to get myself to work each day.

'A succession of models followed this original purchase — BSA, Jawa, Vespa and the infamous Honda Dream, which I virtually gave away. Now it's a collector's item. All of this in the pursuit of reliability and a bit of quality.

'Somewhere about then my life went into some sort of time warp, because before I knew it I was married with two neat little girls, but even they grew up while I wasn't looking. I had worked pretty hard building a business but the fun factor needed to be kick started. This nagging feeling inside me led me to various motorcycle showrooms. The rest, really, is history, because once you have motorcycling in your blood it is there forever!

'In 1990 I purchased my first Harley-Davidson. It was a 1990 FLST black Softail. This led me to the inaugural meeting of the Auckland chapter of the Harley owners group (HOG) and the unfolding of a whole new world and, in fact, a new life. I hadn't told my mother that I had another bike after all these years, so when I went to visit my parents in Tokoroa, I just rolled my helmet in the door. My mother promptly quipped, "I thought you'd grown out of those things." I replied, just as quickly, "Mum, I'm just growing into them."'

'At this time I became aware of the annual biker event at Sturgis in South Dakota, in the States. I have been three times now and have toured from El Paso in the south up to Sturgis and back to El Paso. When I got home from that trip I purchased a full Dresser Touring Harley, and, about that time, I became the director of the Auckland chapter of HOG. This group has raised a lot of money and given a lot of time in support of the Muscular Dystrophy Association here in New Zealand, and it sure balances up the freedom we have with the restriction that they have.

1993 Harley-Davidson FLHTC Ultra Classic

90th Anniversary Limited Edition

No. 0266 of 1340 produced worldwide

80 cubic inch (1340cc) as produced by the factory

Ross Pennell

'Nineteen ninety-three was a milestone for Harley Davidson as they celebrated ninety years of production and they released thirteen hundred and forty Ultra Classics worldwide... I was lucky enough to be "Rosco on the spot" and got the only one released in New Zealand. In 1996 I flew this bike to the States and covered sixteen thousand kilometres. Flying into Los Angeles we headed up to San Francisco, from there over to Sturgis and then down to Memphis to check if Elvis was home (we heard he was pouring gas at the BP station in Te Puke — bugger!). We continued down to "Nu Orleens" then on to Austin, Texas, to Taos, New Mexico and across to Las Vegas. We met up with other HOG members on the way, staying with them and sharing the motorcycle experience. What a trip.

'Through this extended family I have ridden bikes in Australia, Hong Kong, Germany, Italy, Austria and the States.

'Somewhere around this time I managed to acquire a 1942 WLA Harley-Davidson. With a lot of patience and a few bucks I now have a very reliable motorbike. I have just completed a four thousand kilometre round trip to Bluff and joined up with the National Vintage Motorcycle Rally in Dunedin. What I like about the old Harley is that you don't have to hurry, as you are already there. Anyway, if you ride too fast you get there too quickly, and then you have to look for somewhere else to go.

'A bloke asked me the other day what the bike was worth. I told him that it was not for sale and it didn't have a quantifiable value. He went away still trying to put a dollar value on what is an emotional relationship.

'I still get out for rides on the twisty Northland roads at every opportunity. Inside every older person is a younger person wondering what the hell happened.'

1945 Harley-Davidson WLA Solo Civilian

750cc (45 cubic inch)

Allan Ryan
My reserve tank is a two-gallon beer keg

'**As I approached forty** it became obvious to me that I needed an escape from the serious side of life. One look at the prices of large motorcycles convinced me that there had to be a better way. I needed to escape, but there was the small matter of being able to afford to. Thus, the trike was born . . .

'It started life as a VW car, but it didn't take long to mangle it, add to it and give it a new lease of life. For the last four years I have been developing and fine-tuning my creation, doing most of the work during the winter months when I take the trike off the road. At present it has a 1993 eighteen hundred cc Legacy motor, a VW gearbox, axles and a leading link front end. The main fuel tanks are Harley-Davidson Fatboys and my reserve tank is a two-gallon beer keg! I injured my back a while ago so comfort is important. I tow a small trailer with all the creature comforts I need. I usually end up carrying stuff for other guys as well.

'My wife, Trina, and I run a bed-and-breakfast in Te Anau on State Highway 94, and folk are welcome to drop in and see the beast. Each November we organise our own rally at home with a poker run to Milford Sound.

'The trike is a totally unique machine. It allows me to express my individuality. The machine is always "evolving" — this winter, for example, I shall work on making the passenger seat more comfortable for Trina. She travels with me when she can, although with two small children it's not always possible. I haven't managed to persuade her to take the controls yet; she likes to just sit there and gaze at the scenery.'

Asked for her opinion of the trike, Trina grinned and said, 'You have to have a lot of patience. Something or other is always going wrong or falling off. You get to meet a lot of people in garages or by the side of the road. But I enjoy it, really. The trike is Allan's pride and joy.'

Custom-built bike

1993 1800cc Subaru Legacy engine

V.W. gearbox

Harley-Davidson Fatboy fuel tanks

Mark Edmonds

At school it was every boy's dream to have a Norton Commando

In 1983, by then extremely ill, Mark was given a new lease of life with a kidney transplant. The donated kidney functioned perfectly for some eight years, but then Mark became aware that all was not as it should be. Mark's brother was able to come to the rescue and valiantly donated one of his own kidneys, enabling Mark to have a second life-saving transplant.

'It makes you think of all the things you were going to do and you realise you haven't done any of them.'

Since then Mark has got married, bought a house, set up his own real estate business, started a family and rekindled his schoolboy passion for owning and riding motorcycles. For his fortieth birthday he treated himself to the Norton 850 Commando Interstate in the photograph. Back in his school days, when Mark began riding motorcycles, a 125cc bike was thought of as a big machine. A 250cc motorcycle was considered huge. Now, at the Auckland branch of the Ulysses Club where Mark has recently become a junior member, the majority of motorbikes are at least 1000cc and some are as big as 1500cc.

'Back at school it was every boy's dream to own a Norton Commando. When I purchased this one it had had a total engine rebuild and a new paint job. It looked stunning and I couldn't resist. But it developed a bad knocking noise in the motor even as I was riding it home from the shop.'

The engine was stripped down and the offending noise was found to be a seized piston. Apparently, when the rebuild was done and the engine rebored, the piston clearance on one cylinder was insufficient, resulting in the seizure. After a couple of weeks in the workshop, and many hundreds of dollars later, Mark says the bike is now running like a new one.

Mark's aim now is to encourage his friends to re-live their youth and buy motorcycles so they can have their own private club.

'I'm probably more fortunate than most guys because my wife, Sue, has a passion for riding as well and accompanies me on all the rallies and weekends away. Her great attitude has enabled me to buy two bikes and I'm now looking for a third. We hope to take our three-year-old daughter, Lauren, for rides as soon as she is able to hang on!'

1975 Mark 3 Norton Commando Interstate

Engine: 828cc parallel twin

Modification: single instead of twin carburettor

Andre & Kyle Smith
I really like the noise and going fast

It's hardly surprising that brothers Andre and Kyle Smith, aged sixteen and ten years respectively, are already ardent motorcycle enthusiasts. The family pedigree speaks for itself: Dad has had several motorcycles; Mum's side of the family are all involved in either motorcycle sport or leisure riding; one uncle is a founder member of the Kiwi Trikers; another uncle races on the New Zealand race circuit; Grandad has had road bikes for many years and still owns four, including a race bike; Mum has recently got her motorcycle licence and is in the process of building a trike for road use . . . the list goes on and on.

The boys' dad, Kevin, decided to encourage the boys to ride off-road from an early age. That way, he reasoned, they could be taught to ride safely and well, in a controlled environment and in the company of other bike enthusiasts. Mum was also full of encouragement and was on hand to watch the boys racing.

Kyle
'I like the smell of the motorbike fumes and the cool wind in my face and I really like the noise and going fast. I started riding a 50cc bike at Nan and Pop's house when I was five years old. I started motocross on a Suzuki DS80I. I competed in the Rodney Mini race and got a trophy! I enjoy riding on my own in the sand or on dirt tracks. I wear lots of safety gear — gloves, boots, a chest protector, a kidney belt, special bike pants. It means that Mum and Dad don't have to worry about me getting hurt and I can enjoy my riding. I am in Year Six at Stanmore Bay Primary School in Auckland. I don't know where my motorbike riding will take me. For now it's just fun . . . but who knows?'

Andre
'Motorcycles have always been a passion of mine, right from the age of seven when I used to ride my Pop's 50cc Honda. I've always loved riding on the back of my uncle's motorbike, too. Now that I'm sixteen, I'm hoping Dad will let me get my own licence.

'I got my first competitive motocross bike when I was twelve. It was awesome — a 1989 KX-80 Big Wheel. I learnt to ride in Woodhill Forest. From that bike I stepped up to a Honda XL185 four-stroke and then on to a KDX200 Enduro bike two-stroke, which was a lot of fun. I prefer two-stroke bikes, they're louder and have a faster pick-up. The power in these little bikes is incredible. These days I'm riding a 1997 KX80 II Big Wheel, which is an excellent little bike.

'I really love motorcycles, mainly I suppose because I have been brought up with them, they have always been part of my life.'

Andre's bike:
Kawasaki KX80 II Big Wheel
2-stroke, single cylinder
Weight: 66 kg
Disc brakes
6-speed constant mesh transmission
Pro Circuit exhaust
USD (upside down) forks
80cc engine capacity
Height: 1.08 metres
Kick start
Petrol: oil mix 32:1

Kyle's bike
Kawasaki KX60
2-stroke, single cylinder
Weight: 50 kg
Drum brakes
6-speed constant mesh transmission
Height: 0.915 metres
60cc engine capacity
Kick start
Petrol: oil mix 32:1

Bruce Anderson

These little Harleys . . . have been a lifetime interest for me

Bruce Anderson has been involved in the world of motorcycles from a very young age. His father, F.V. (Vic) Anderson, started a motor repair business behind the family home in Remuera, Auckland, in 1933. When the business moved to 305 Remuera Road in 1945 young Bruce began his apprenticeship. Taking over the business on his father's retirement, Bruce put in a sterling 41 years before retiring himself in 1986. The building in Remuera is now a restaurant, not surprisingly known as 305. The number 305, incidentally, is also Bruce's motorcycle racing number.

Over the years Bruce's passion for classic motorcycles has led him on an unrelenting search for genuine parts with which to restore these wonderful old machines to their former glory. His painstaking and meticulous research has led him to correspond with other devotees and from such correspondence lasting friendships have been forged.

'I joined the Auckland Branch of the Vintage Car Club in its inception year and for nearly twenty years, before the group had its own clubrooms, promoted the motorcycle section with monthly meetings and annual swap meets at my garage premises in Remuera Road. I rode a 1926 side-valve 350 Harley-Davidson "Pup" for many years in rallies and club events, and later on a 1927 OHV350. I remember I paid the grand sum of one pound for the "Pup" — it was in pieces and the gearbox was missing. I had to pay three pounds for another frame with a gearbox in it! These little Harleys were produced from 1925 to 1934 and have been a lifetime interest for me. My personal associations with old-time racing riders of the 1920s enabled me to acquire genuine Harley-Davidson "Works" components to build the racing Peashooter. This little Harley-Davidson has proved to be quite competitive in the 350cc Vintage-class races at the Pukekohe track.'

Another testimony to Bruce's restoration skills is the Mark 8 KTT Velocette powered by engine number 1030, shown in the second photograph. This bike, too, has a very interesting history; it won the Belgian Grand Prix in 1948 and achieved second place in the Isle of Man Junior TT that same year, with Bob Foster in the saddle. The KTT might well have won the Junior TT, but the gearbox belts worked loose and tightened the primary chain which in turn flogged out the two rear engine bolts. Velocette race mechanic Frank Panes bored and resleeved the two holes and it was these very repairs which enabled the KTT to be positively identified years

Replica 1929 Harley-Davidson 350cc Peashooter TT

Special racing 2-port cylinder head

Steel flywheels

Racing cams

Timing case and oil pump

Roller cam-followers

11:1 compression ratio

Early brass TT carburettor jetted for methanol

Three-speed, hand-change gearbox

Bruce Anderson

later. Some marvellous detective work followed, including the retrieval of the factory drawing of the gearbox and notes made by Frank Panes himself. In 1954 the Velocette was shipped to Sydney, where it was ridden by Bob Brown, who finished second to Rod Coleman and his 7R at Bathurst. After that the machine was raced extensively in Australia before being brought to New Zealand in the 1960s.

By the time Bruce managed to buy it in 1995, the Velocette was nothing more than a collection of parts. True to form, Bruce set out to build and restore this very special piece of motorcycling history to its original state. With the cooperation of Rod Coleman, Chris North and Steve Raffils, and with the use of original factory drawings, the frame and forks were reproduced. Bruce himself made the oil tank and added the correct Andre damper, Dunlop saddle and oleomatic rear suspension units. Bob Jolly supplied new magnesium hubs. Bruce machined the fittings for a new fuel tank, the tank itself being made by Steve Roberts from patterns for the original. Cycle Colour then enamelled it and, as you can see from the photograph, the Velocette is now fully restored and in 'ready to race' condition. Classic motorcycle enthusiasts may well have seen this amazing machine proudly completing eight laps of the Pukekohe track in October 1999.

Bruce's wife, Maureen, has managed *not* to get involved with her husband's hobby. 'Maureen doesn't like motorbikes,' chuckles Bruce. His son Malcolm, however, is following in Bruce's footsteps. Malcolm Anderson has recorded many successes racing his father's meticulously restored motorcycles.

Other 350cc Harleys owned within the family are a 1926 OHV grass-track racer, a 1927 magneto model OHV with carbide lighting, and a 1928 side valve machine.

Mark 8 KTT Velocette

Engine number 1030

Oleomatic suspension

Magnesium hubs

Scavange pump

Malcolm Baird

I have steadily improved on the necessary comforts for roughing it

Malcolm had some less than comfortable experiences before he perfected the art of turning his motorcycle into a pantechnicon.

'Imagine the scene. Snow six inches deep on the ground. One standard four-man tent. Inside, three blokes on foam mats with barely adequate sleeping bags. This was my first experience of a motorcycle rally, the Brass Monkey, back in 1982!

'Since then, I have steadily improved on the necessary comforts for roughing it. Food preparation is much easier with the addition of a folding table with separate stools. Spring-tension folding chairs were already a feature in the load. I tried stretchers for a while and I still use them with extra warm self-inflating foam mats for the Brass Monkey Rally (that space underneath gets rather cold). In the last few years, however, an inflatable double air bed has been the answer for sleeping comfort. The tent, of course, has grown. I decided we might as well have plenty of room to stand up, so a six-man dome tent holds us and our gear quite comfortably.

'There is always something new coming on the market to make life easier, so a two-seater blow-up couch has been added to the essential rally gear. Needless to say my wife, Yvonne, rides her own bike, a 1992 Yamaha XJ600, and helps spread the load, particularly when our two boys come.

'The bike that has taken me — and all the gear — to most places in this motorcycling paradise we call New Zealand, is a 1982 Kawasaki Z1000J. However, after a hundred and eighty-six thousand kilometres, it has now been retired to commuting and lighter duties. In 1995 I replaced the Kawasaki with the Triumph Sprint in the photograph. This new machine has proved to be a worthy successor in every respect, although I can't see it taking me to Macetown or on an adventure route as the old bike did. It is, however, a more stable vehicle with a full load. The old Kawasaki front end used to get a bit light and wobbly at speeds below twenty kilometres an hour. Mind you, the Macetown did not involve luggage. We went two up through twenty-seven fords on the way in, and the same on the way back. Having four cylinders helps when fording, you can lose two and still come out the other side with two under power.

'In the heyday of rally-going (late eighties, early nineties) it was not unusual to do fifteen rallies in a year. Sometimes this meant going away three weekends in a row. The Rusty Nuts Thousand Mile Run was always a three thousand kilometre weekend, away Friday morning and home again in the early hours of Monday. The Brass Monkey has been a "must do" for the last eighteen years.'

1995 Triumph Sprint 900

3 cylinders, 885cc capacity, liquid cooled

Fuel tank: 25 litre capacity, range 300–350 km

Dry weight: 215 kg

Loaded weight: 370 kg

Tyres: Dunlop Radial

Extended front guard

Sue & Warren Gibbons

It's a great way to see the country

They are almost identical twins — the bikes, that is. The only difference between them is that Sue's BMW has a picture of a bumblebee on the windscreen and the seat is a bit lower. Like many twins, the pair are inseparable. Even the chassis numbers are consecutive, proving that the bikes have been together since birth, so to speak. The 'twin thing' was almost inevitable really: Warren and Sue are the proud parents of twins — a son and daughter, aged 23 years.

Having ridden motorcycles together for over twenty years, Warren and Sue have graduated from farm bikes and motocross to road riding — and they don't do anything by halves. Initially Sue tried to keep up with Warren's Kawasaki GPZ250 on a Yamaha SR250 . . .

'That lasted two weeks. [The Yamaha] didn't go as fast as the GPZ, so it got traded for a Honda VT250. Warren is a pretty big bloke and he fast outgrew the Kawasaki, so he bought another model, this time a GPX500. Thereafter followed a virtual stream of bikes, all of them Kawasakis.'

And so on . . . and on . . . until somehow Warren and Sue ended up with Kawasaki ZZR1100s. They then, of course, decided to swap them for the two lusty BMWs you see in the photograph.

With a feminine eye for detail, Sue has even had her motorcycle leathers hand-painted in grey and yellow to match the bikes.

'The outfit was originally black, white, orange and purple,' she says. 'Can you believe it? I looked like a liquorice allsort. Mind you, the paint is wearing a bit thin on the seat of the trousers. Now the old purple colour is showing through — it looks as though I've got a bum like a baboon!'

In 1991, Warren and Sue joined the Ulysses Club in Auckland. Sue was on the Ulysses Auckland Branch Committee for several years, 'representing the female perspective and also prodding sausages at functions.'

Their love of motorcycling has taken Warren and Sue from Kaitaia to Stewart Island and has introduced them to people from all walks of life.

'It's a great way to see the country — and often challenging — but it creates a bond with fellow riders that only they can understand,' says Warren.

1998 BMW K1200 RS

Fuel injection

6-speed gearbox

Shaft drive

Paul Hanes

I had just had the time of my life

It must be an Indian owner's worst nightmare. When Paul and fellow rider, Brent, both members of the Indian Team New Zealand, dreamed of racing their beloved Indian motorcycles at the famous Daytona race track in 1999, little did they realise what lay ahead.

Indian Team New Zealand was formed in 1997 with the aim of facilitating just such trips to one of the most famous race tracks in the world. With the enthusiastic help of other members of the club, together with some sponsorship, funds were raised to support the venture. After all, this was the first time Indian racers from New Zealand would be represented at such a prestigious venue; Paul and Brent's experiences would provide useful information for the future.

Paul found his bike, similar to the one Ed Kretz rode in the first Daytona 200 race in 1937, in the States in 1990. It was in bits with a lot missing. It had been set up for long track racing (similar to speedway racing on dirt in New Zealand, but with longer tracks). Paul spent four and a half years rebuilding the bike and has since had a huge amount of enjoyment from it. The bike can be a bit of a handful to ride on some of New Zealand's smaller, tighter circuits but, says Paul, it loves Puke, especially the long back straight. Before this bike, Paul had never raced on the tarseal. He has raced at most North Island tracks, on the beach at Christchurch and, of course, at Daytona.

'With our entries to the races at Daytona accepted, we flew out to Los Angeles and from there down to Daytona via Atlanta. The next day we all piled into a little hire car and headed down to Orlando to pick up the bikes. The bikes had not arrived and the freight company didn't seem to know where they were. After hanging round for a couple of hours we went back to our hotel and starting making phone calls. Still no luck. The next day, it was back to the freight company, but still there was no news. I felt quite sick not knowing where the love of my life was. We even appealed to the New Zealand Embassy in Washington for help. Things got quite heated — you can imagine our frustration — but to cut a long story short the freight company eventually located our bikes in San Francisco, of all places. What a nightmare! But the drama still wasn't over.

'The bikes had to be flown from San Francisco to Miami and then trucked to Orlando. I think the crate must have had a sign on it saying, "Please mess us around", as then it was the turn of the US Customs to play their part.

1938 Indian Sports Scout Racer

Bore and stroke: 2 7/8 x 3

Gearbox: Indian 3-speed

Foot clutch

Hand shift

750cc (45 cubic inch)

Side valve engine

18" wheels

Single Linkert carburettor

Dry sump oil

Paul Hanes

By the time we got possession of the bikes, it was almost too late. The Deland races were all over. These races are used as preliminary races before Daytona; it's really at the Deland races that the bikes are sorted out and given their handicap ratings. The races are held on the Deland airport runways, which were built during the war. The track is basically a series of long straights with sharp corners. This was the first time we were to meet the American Indian racers, but of course we missed out on the racing and, equally importantly, on the pre-race practice. You can't race without a bike.

'We got our bikes just in time for the Daytona races. By the time we had unpacked the bikes from the crate and put them together it was time to go. We were told to be in line outside the track at three a.m. ready for the gates to open at seven. Those few hours standing around in the dark and cold seemed to last for ever. Then it was time to enter this famous track. Down through the tunnel we went, under the track to the infield.

'My jaw fell open, that place was huge. We didn't have much time left as we were on at eight for practice. We had received a lot of advice on how to ride the banking at Daytona, like "go high, it's faster". Well, let me tell you, my first time out I went high, right up close to the concrete wall, but I could not keep the bike at ninety degrees to the track, or keep a good line. The bike kept wanting to go down the bank. What with riding on an angle, thinking the bike was going to slip off, not being able to keep a good line and being so high up, my brain was telling me it wasn't right. After practice, I felt I couldn't handle the banks. We didn't have long to wait for the pre-forty race. With my gear on, waiting to go into the dummy grid, I had a chance to think about this three point nine mile long circuit — and, boy, was I nervous.

'Once we got moving on the warm-up lap I felt better, then it was back to the starting grid. I got a bad start, which is normal when I am nervous. On the first lap I went round the banking at about ten feet from the bottom, this felt a lot better. The banks are a straight thirty-three degrees from bottom to top. I know this doesn't sound steep, but when you are riding it, it feels almost vertical. After a lap or so I was starting to feel more comfortable and was able to start passing and making my way through the field. I managed to get a fifth placing which, in my first race, really pleased me. After crossing the finish line and doing one slow lap, I led the field back to the dummy grid. Before I had a chance to stop I had a microphone jammed in my helmet and a guy started asking me heaps of questions. I was really stuffed and my mouth was so dry I could hardly speak. How could I explain that I had just had the time of my life? Since they give plaques down to sixth place, I have now got a chunk of wood from Daytona on my wall. It might only be a piece of wood, but it means the world to me!'

Noel Messer

You should ride to live, so you can live to ride

'**I don't really care what people ride**, so long as they love it, look after it, and it gets their knees in the breeze.'

So says 48-year-old Noel Messer, also known as the Wizard of Oz, originally from Australia but now loving life in New Zealand. His love of motorcycles has lasted through two marriages, four children and four grandchildren. As for bikes, Noel has owned them all — from Yamahas, Hondas and Kawasakis to Panthers, Triumphs, BSAs and Harley-Davidsons.

Equally fond of tattoos, there aren't many parts of Noel's anatomy that haven't been thus decorated. Noel himself has been practicing the art of tattooing for over twelve years.

'Yes, of course it hurts. A Samoan did the ones on my bum. The chisel went almost through to the bone!'

Noel has a fondness for long front ends, fishtail mufflers and American muscle cars. He has his own 1978 Pontiac TransAm.

But trikes are his first love and, if all goes according to plan, Noel will be manufacturing trikes for sale here in New Zealand before too long. Noel's latest trike is entirely hand built by Noel himself using a range of parts from Volkswagen, Harley-Davidson and Subaru. He is currently busy building a trike for girlfriend Kelly (he has also covered her in tattoos). The new trike will have a stainless steel beer keg for a fuel tank. According to the Wizard of Oz, the key to a good trike is the frame and the front suspension. Noel had just this conversation with comedian Billy Connolly — another trike devotee — when the star stopped to admire Noel's trike on the road in Australia.

Safety is a key issue for Noel: 'You should ride to live, so you can live to ride. One of the great things about a trike is that it doesn't fall down in the wet.

'And if you're into being noticed . . .'

Custom-built bike
Engine: Subaru 1600cc
Weight: 450 kg

Roger des Forges

I love the smell of mud and two-stroke fumes

A dairy farmer for many years, Roger has been an orchardist since 1980, growing kiwi fruit, or Zespri as they have become known. Off-roading is his passion, a sport which, he says, goes hand in hand with farming.

'I bought my first bike in 1972, a Suzuki T350. Then I discovered trail riding. I bought myself an XR400 and I'm now secretary of the Thames Valley Motorcycle Club, which devotes itself to dirt bikes, motocross and trail riding.

'I used to love riding in the Enduro competitions. Usually the races were about a hundred and forty kilometres off-road. One race — the Virgin Swamps Enduro — at Riverhead Forest, north of Auckland, was just a wet, sticky mess. Muddy as . . . but great fun! The Woodhill Enduro was all over sand dunes and on the beach. It was a real challenge to do the Enduro rides. You had to be tough just to finish one. Nowadays they've gone soft. In the late 1970s we used to have about a hundred and fifty starters. Out of those, only about fifteen riders even managed to finish the course. The others got stuck on the hills and were subsequently "houred out". Put simply, this meant that they had run out of time. Each section of the race had a time allowance allocated to it; if you didn't complete a section quickly enough you were penalised or even disqualified. Enduro riding is a great sport. I love the smell of mud and two-stroke fumes — just beautiful.

'In 1982 I won the Suzuki Series of Enduro races on a DR250 Z. I reckon Enduro riding goes well with farming. As a farmer, you're out in all weathers and on all kinds of terrain. I use a bike on the farm in any case. Farming and off-road motorcycles go hand in hand.

'My wife Sandra hates biking and so doesn't come with me. We've got four daughters and it's nice to escape from five women on occasion. If I don't get on that bike at least once a week I get withdrawal symptoms. I start thrashing the car.

'I must confess to loving speed. Believe it or not, though, I got my first ticket for speeding in 1998 — after twenty-nine years of motorcycling. I'd only just bought the VFR800 and I reckon it rather ran away with me.'

Honda VFR800

Engine: Liquid-cooled 4-stroke 16-valve

Bore and stroke: 72 x 48 mm

Displacement: 781.7cc

Compression ratio: 11.6:1

Carburation: electronic direct fuel injection

Transmission: 6-speed

Fuel capacity: 21 litres

Dry weight: 208 kg

Ian Robertson & Mamta
I like everything about bikes

When we met Ian Robertson, handsome veterinarian-cum-televison presenter, and his lovely lady, Mamta, it didn't take us long to realise that Ian is simply passionate about both Mamta and his Harley-Davidson.

'I've been riding motorcycles since my university days. I started out on a Yamaha SR250, much the same as the bike Mamta currently owns. I owned other bikes and then eventually I bought my first Harley. Some people, I know, still see Harley riders as having a "bad boy" image, and I suppose I look quite the picture when I'm in my full leathers with face mask and black helmet. But I prefer to look on the Harley as a ticket to "extra good boys' time"! It's a time to wear jeans and leather, grow my beard and swot up on all my jokes.

And there have been some incredible adventures, including the trip of a lifetime along what's left of Route 66 in the States. The journey included Canada and most of the Western USA, through Vegas, the Grand Canyon, Mount Rushmore, Bryce Canyon, the Black Hills and Sturgis. It was an absolutely awesome experience.

'The motto I live by is: "Live life the way you'll wish you had lived it when you're sitting in your rocking chair". That trip to the States was one I'll definitely remember from my rocking chair.

'What do I like about bikes? I like *everything* about bikes, but particularly Harley-Davidsons. There's an old Harley saying, something along the lines of "If you have to ask, you wouldn't understand." The sound (potato, potato, potato — say it quickly and it mimics the sound of a Harley sitting at the lights), the look, the feel, the fact that all your senses are involved as you move your body, smell the air, hear the sound of your bike, see the world without car doors in the way, and even taste the occasional bug. We've all heard the old saying about "boys and their toys" — well, my Harley is *my* toy.

Not that long ago my first Harley was stolen. Disaster! Talk about heartbreak. However, they say everything has a purpose and I'm delighted to say I've got an even better Harley now.

1995 Harley-Davidson Heritage Nostalgia Softail

Ian Robertson & Mamta

'When I met Mamta, it was a case of "Love me, love my bike". Mamta spent many hours getting used to being on the back of my bike then, being Mamta, she decided to go out and buy her own. The lady never ceases to amaze me.

New Zealand law meant she understandably wasn't allowed to learn to ride on a Harley-Davidson, so she bought a Yamaha SR250 and I had the words "I wanna be a Harley-Davidson" printed on the tank! She took to riding like a duck to water and is now hooked on motorcycling. Her colleagues at work even had a special name-plate made for her — it simply says: "MAMTA — BIKER CHICK".

'Eventually she'll get her own Harley. Mamta doesn't know the colour yet, but she's hoping it's going to be purple — to match her purple Doc Martin boots.'

Yamaha SR250

Eric & Carol Smith

There was always a bike of one sort or another in the shed

'**My first powered machine** was a push-bike which I fitted with a two-stroke motor. I was only fourteen at the time and was well pleased with my efforts. The downside was the need to get a licence. I had to bend the truth a bit about my age and I was lucky to come across a really friendly traffic officer. It's amazing what a bit of charm will do.

'My first real motorcycle was a BSA Bantam 150cc. It was really awesome. I remember managing to get up to a speed of fifty miles per hour — going downhill, of course. Then came a whole assortment of bikes, from Norton Ariels to Jawas. Interestingly, I first met my wife-to-be changing the plugs on her Norton Dominator by the side of the road. Yes, I managed to rescue a damsel in distress!

'We married a few years later and children put motorcycling out of the picture for a few years. Then in the 1970s, when possum skins were of value, I decided I needed a decent machine to go possuming. A dirt bike fitted the bill and from there, of course, the bikes just got bigger and bigger. There was always a bike of one sort or another in the shed. When the kids left home to start their own lives, Carol and I were able to really get into motorcycling again. Carol bought a Suzuki Intruder 800 and I had an old BMW.

'My other lifetime ambition was to visit Alaska. I started saving up for the trip and put money aside regularly. Then came decision time. There was I in a motorcycle shop, just browsing, like you do. I happened to pick up a pamphlet on the Suzuki VL1500 Intruder. The damage was done! I really liked the look of the bike. It had just the styling I liked and the specifications were exactly what I wanted. It was hard, it really was, but I knew it had to be one or the other — the trip to Alaska or the bike. Decisions, decisions. As you've probably guessed by now, the bike won. I've never regretted the decision, it means I can see the whole of New Zealand in style. In any case, it's better than freezing my arse off in the snow and ice. My bike is a bit like Alaska though — big, bold and beautiful.

Eric's bike:

Suzuki VL1500 Intruder

1462cc

Engine: air-cooled 45-degree V-Twin OHC 3-valve

Compression ratio: 8.5:1

5-speed transmission

Brakes: disc, front and rear

Fuel tank capacity: 15.5 litres

Wheel base: 1700 mm

Dry weight: 296 kg

Carol's bike:

Suzuki Intruder 800

Engine: water-cooled V-Twin 2-cylinder

Compression ratio: 10.0:1

5-speed transmission

Front brakes: disc

Rear brakes: hydraulic internal expanding, mechanically operated

Fuel tank capacity: 12 litres

Neil Sheeran

I started riding my dad's bike when I was eleven

'**My interest in motorcycles** really came from my grandfather, Allan Charlton. Grandad was the co-owner of a motorcycle shop called Skeates and White in the Khyber Pass area of Auckland. I used to love going to the shop. I started riding my dad's bike when I was eleven years old. Mind you, Dad didn't approve. He didn't even know about it. I used to push Dad's Triumph Speedtwin out of the garage and halfway across Henderson so that Dad wouldn't hear it start! Dad was forever tuning the bike, wondering what on earth was wrong with the fuel economy. I got my own bike when I was thirteen, a 1952 Triumph Spring Hub and I've had almost every model of Triumph since then.

'In 1972 I went over to Australia and co-founded the Lithgow Motorcycle Club with my friend, Don Compagnoni. I acted as secretary for two years, organising competitions and generally running the club. Don and I went on to start the Lithgow Police Citizens Boys' Club Riding School which fostered several Australian off-road champions. We weren't far from Bathurst, so it's hardly surprising I developed an interest in competitive motorcycling. I managed to win the Forest 300 twice while I was in Australia as well as the Lance Watson race, and I won gold medals in three open class two-day endurance races. However, I stopped racing when Don, my best mate, mentor and sponsor, was killed on his motorcycle.

'In 1994 I returned to New Zealand and my interest in motorcycles was rekindled. I bought a Honda CBR600 as a wreck and put it back together. I went on to buy a 1991 Suzuki Intruder 1400. My partner, Fay, can ride pillion on the Intruder, whereas the Honda CBR is really a one-man bike. Just to round out my interest I've also started a business manufacturing motorcycle parts in New Lynn in Auckland.

'In my racing days, I managed to break every bone in my left foot and my right ankle twice. The second time I broke my ankle I was entered in a big event in Australia and I still managed to win the race.

'I've travelled all over Australia on my motorcycle. One of the events I entered started at sea level and ended at the Rocky Mountains. I remember I once ran over a kangaroo and broke its leg. When I turned up at a vet's place at eleven o'clock at night he was none too pleased — kangaroos are regarded as pests over there.'

1991 Suzuki Intruder 1400

1400cc V-Twin

Harry Lawler

My first bike was a Sunbeam, which I purchased for ten pounds

As the oldest motorcyclist in our book, Harry Lawler, 93 years young, has many a fine tale to tell about his early years as a motorcycle devotee, including the following true story of an incident which occurred on a trip to Pukekohe.

'I was travelling with my fiancée on the pillion. She tapped me on the shoulder and said, "There is a man waving his arms because he needs help and wants you to stop." Being the nice sort of fellow that I am, I duly stopped . . . but all I received for my efforts was a traffic ticket. It turned out that the "man" was a traffic inspector!

'I started racing push-bikes in 1921, including track cycling at Auckland Domain, in front of the present Grandstand area, and road racing from Hamilton to Auckland on a fixed wheel machine. In those days the road surface was just gravel, all the way. I used to race against Slater Hayes and Tim Lowndes. In the late 1920s I graduated to motorcycles. My first bike was a Sunbeam, which I purchased for ten pounds.

'Later I bought myself a Chater-Lea with a Blackburne engine. I used the machine both for racing and for personal transport. I even used it for grass-track racing on the Takapuna Race Course. This area, adjacent to Auckland's Takapuna Grammar School, is now a golf course. Competitors in those days included Percy Coleman (father of Rod Coleman) on his Harley-Davidson, Harry Mangam on his Indian, Oscar Shakespeare on his Excelsior Big X and myself, of course, on the Chater-Lea/Blackburne. Later I raced at Hennings Speedway at Mangere during the day and at Western Springs, when it first opened, in the evenings. I had an early 350cc Velocette with hand-change.

'Before the Second World War, from about 1935 until 1940, I spent my time designing, building and racing speed-boats. During one race from Point Chevalier to North Head, my boats exploded and burnt to the water-line. I jumped overboard and nearly drowned as I couldn't swim.

'After the war I started a carrying business and became well known as "The Potato King". I was still interested in boats but, after building several small boats, my interest then turned to motorcycles. I started a collection of mopeds and continental scooters. I still have about sixteen of them in various stages of restoration. I recently gave up riding motorcycles. I suppose at my age you have to stop, but I still have my car licence so I can still drive myself around.'

Puch Scooters

125cc and 150cc

3-speed gears on handlebars

Flywheel Magneto ignitions

DKW Hobby Scooter

125cc

Automatic transmission

Brian Clearkin

After a mere twenty-four year interlude I was born-again as a biker

'**I discovered motorcycles** and girls when I was about sixteen. Motorcycling started with the frequently compromised joys of a Francis Barnett 98cc autocycle and progressed to a deeply committed relationship with a 650cc Ariel Huntmaster twin. However, the girlfriends progressed through to a wife and family and, alas, the bike was replaced with a twin tub Hoovermatic full of nappies.

'After a mere twenty-four year interlude I was born again as a biker on a Z1100 Kawasaki Four. This, plus an XV1000 Yamaha, and a small collection of trail bikes, kept me smiling until I found a merlot red 1993 Triumph Trophy Four, which I traded two years later for the British racing green 1994 model I am currently riding.

'I have found motorcycling to be an educational as well as an enjoyable pastime. The fundamentals of physics are easily studied on wet roads, tram tracks and tight corners. I remember one youthful flying lesson hanging upside down in mid air with a Matchless 350cc single in hot pursuit. Fortunately, in the absence of a crash helmet, I got off lightly — nothing worse than a broken arm. Philosophical enlightenment also accompanied the conjunction of heavy rain and inadequate wet weather gear when far from home: "Some are born to stoicism whilst others have stoicism thrust upon them."

'I enjoy sharing my love of riding. I have even taken my eighty-five-year-old father for a cruise down Auckland's southern motorway. My five sons have wide-ranging views on motorbikes, but only the youngest is currently a rider. My other passions include sailing (I have a seventeen-foot Mystere-class catamaran) and marathon running. In addition to riding most days of the week, I enjoy the simple pleasures of life including good company, good music, red wine and pasta.'

Brian is also a member of the Auckland branch of the Ulysses Motorcycle Club, membership of which is restricted to those over 40 years of age.

'I look forward to weekend rallies with the Ulysses club. At these gatherings I am often seen wearing the navy and red "kepi" of my alter ego Capitaine Jean-Claude Delacroix — an impeccably gallant ex-*officier de la Legion d'Etrangere*! While Jean-Claude has significantly diminished my wine supplies, I would like to point out that not a single franc has been offered towards their replacement.'

1994 Triumph Trophy 4 1200

Engine: liquid-cooled DOHC, in-line 4-cylinder

1180cc

Bore and stroke: 76 by 36 mm

Compression ratio: 10.6 :1

Carburettors: 4 by 36mm flat side CV

Maximum power: 108 PS at 9000 rpm

Maximum torque: 104 Nm at 5000 rpm

Maximum revs: 9700 rpm

Gary Soden

The original bike was so very ugly that I had to change it

'**When I was young**, the Mad Max movies had a great effect on my brain. I could not concentrate at school. I would stare out of the window dreaming of sadistic-looking bikes with flaming exhausts. After leaving school I worked as a well driller. I used to have to visit large pulp and paper mills. Once again the heavy industrial atmosphere greatly affected my brain. This led to an obsession with Norwegian Black Metal music which, after years of mind trips and hallucinations, eventually led to the construction of my motorcycle.

'I bought the motorcycle from my brother for five hundred dollars after he had ridden it around the South Island on three cylinders. I fixed the head and rode it in "standard" form for a short while, but the original bike was so very ugly that I had to change it.

'My friends say I'm only here while my home planet is being cleaned. My response to that is that I like my planet dirty! I have passed cars on the road on this bike and have watched as they almost run off the road laughing at me. This is good.'

Driving around Lake Taupo on a wet and misty morning was in itself a fairly spooky experience. But that was nothing compared to meeting Mad Max in his lair. What from the outside looks like a fairly normal Kiwi dwelling is on the inside more like a medieval castle — four-poster beds, huge chandeliers and Gothic-looking sculptures, fulfilling the promise of the extraordinary bike parked outside.

GSX750 ESD

Stucci race fairing: found in the back of a mate's wood shed

Custom exhaust: Peter Mackly of Custom Chambers

Tellis vacuum tubes: found under car body at local dump

Fluffy fairing fur: supplied by a road-killed rabbit

Shortend frame: cut down in shed with gas axe after too many beers

Wheel covers: stolen from scrap pile at rear of local sheet metal factory

Low seat: cut down with bread knife borrowed from mother-in-law

Crank case: thanks to New Zealand Breweries for empty Waikato can

Ton Hilhorst

A sidecar outfit handles like a pig on roller skates

Ton Hilhorst arrived in New Zealand from Holland in 1975. His lifelong love of motorcycles has led him from a German Zundapp 125cc, which he rode in Holland during the early 1970s, to his present motorcycle and sidecar outfit, a BMW R1100 RT. Along the way Ton has also been the owner of a Honda GL1000, a Honda 500, four Harley-Davidson Shovelheads and several BMW R100 RTs.

'When I first came to New Zealand I toured the North and South Islands for several months on a Honda GL1000. It was one of the first of its kind in New Zealand. I've been into sidecar outfits, though, for the last twelve years. My present outfit, the one in the photograph, has travelled a hundred and twenty thousand kilometres since 1996.

'I work in the hospitality industry as a restaurant manager and so I usually have to work at weekends. I do all my motorcycle riding on weekdays. My work means I am unable to attend a lot of the motorcycle rallies, but I do get out there. People often ask me why I prefer a motorcycle and sidecar. Well, you either love them or hate them: "A sidecar outfit handles like a pig on roller skates, but somehow you never have so much fun." Then, too, people are always shocked when I tell them the cost. "Ah," they say, "You could buy a nice car or boat for that price." Well, you could also buy forty thousand rolls of toilet paper!

'If you know your restrictions with a sidecar and the outfit is properly set up, you can cover a long distance in a day. And I give a lot of solo riders a run for their money on the back roads and twisties. Most people have respect and admire how an outfit is handled. It doesn't really matter what you ride — be it a solo bike, a sidecar outfit or a trike — as long as you are out there enjoying the freedom. I often go out for a "coffee ride", which somehow ends up as a five hundred or eight hundred kilometre "day ride". I suppose that is how I manage to average about thirty thousand kilometres a year. The only reason I stop when I am out on my own is to fill up with gas every three hundred kilometres. I ride in all weather conditions, but I love spring and autumn the best. It is not where or when you arrive that counts — it is making the journey. I was once without a bike for three months, and I had withdrawal symptoms. I hope I never have to go through that again.'

BMW R1100

Engine: 4-stroke

Customised EZS subframe

EZS leading link forks

Tyre size, front and rear 165/70 14"

Sidecar: EZS TPGL

Length: 2260 mm

Width: 1020 mm

Height: 1000 mm

Dry weight: 95 kg

Boot capacity: 300 litres

Frame: rigid tubular steel with bonded rubber anti-vibration fail-safe body mountings. Koni shock absorber and disc brake.

Top speed: 175 kmph

Fuel consumption: 6.7 L/100 km

Jared Scorgie

The bike still has its original death-defying sixteen-inch front wheel

'I bought the Moto Guzzi as a 1987 Mark IV Le Mans 1000. It was second-hand and had travelled just over eight thousand kilometres. Over the next seven years I managed to take the total to ninety thousand kilometers, the reason being that the Guzzi was my only transport — I had no car, no car licence or driving experience. At that stage I re-ringed and re-bearinged the motor. The result was three more years of hard riding and another eighty thousand kilometres on the clock. By then the machine was in need of a complete rebuild, the final result being the motorcycle in the photograph.

'Yes, the bike still has its original death-defying sixteen-inch front wheel. I fitted low, wide handlebars to keep the weight forward, good tyres, a steering dampener and heavier front springs. This makes the bike more stable over bumpy ground at speed than some of the newer Guzzi models I have ridden.

'Over the hundred and seventy thousand kilometres the Guzzi was very reliable and great to ride. I am looking forward to another hundred and seventy thousand kilometres in modified form. It's great to think I have been able to do all the modifications myself.

'Each year, for the past six years, I have organised a get-together for the New Zealand Moto Guzzi Riders. We meet up at a different venue each year, alternating between the South and North Islands. Usually we manage to get sixty or seventy people together for a barbeque and a ride. I've even been known to hand out a few trophies to the best riders.'

1987 Moto Guzzi Mark IV Le Mans 1050

Engine: 2-valve push rod, single cam

92 mm barrel (88 mm standard)

Dyna coils

Corillo rods

Lightened balanced crank

G.G. aluminium single plate clutch flywheel

Straight cut timing gears

C.S.L. race cam, valve springs

Mikuni 40 mm race carburettors

Derek Riddell

Touring motorcycles don't get much better than this

Derek is one of many motorcyclists who, for family and financial reasons, was only able to 'indulge' his passion in later life.

'Like a lot of older motorcyclists, my interest in motorcycles began at an early age. In the early days, the motorcycle was an inexpensive mode of transport and I suppose that was one of the main attractions for me. That and the lack of money. My first motorcycle was purchased in about 1958 for the equivalent of twelve dollars. It was a second-hand Excelsior two-stroke. Then came the getting-married-raising-children-and-large-mortgage era . . . and, of course, there was no money for a motorcycle.

'Then, in my late forties I rediscovered motorcycles. My, how motorcycles have changed over the last twenty-five years or so. Better brakes, better engineering, more comfort, more reliability. After a couple of years of riding with the Ulysses Club I decided it was time to have some of the comforts of life and so purchased a Honda 1200 Gold Wing. Oh, I thought I had gone to heaven! The smooth, quiet power, the built-in panniers and top box, more storage space than I needed . . .

'Twelve months later and life got even better for me. I met Ros, the new lady in my life, and I purchased a Honda Gold Wing 1500. Touring motorcycles don't get much better than this. The 1500 has smooth, reliable power, a radio-cassette player, rider/pillion intercom, enough storage space even for Ros's hairdryer — things have certainly changed since my first Excelsior!

'With all the positive things, however, there were a few negatives. The big one was if the Gold Wing fell over — which it did a couple of times. We found we were unable to lift it up on our own. So, after some deliberation, we decided to convert it to a trike. It was then a matter of getting on the Internet to select which conversion kit we would choose. We decided on a kit from Motor-Trike of Texas, USA. With the help of some friends we dismantled the Gold Wing and assembled the trike. It took about a month in our spare time. The first time out on the trike was a bit scary — it was so unlike a motorcycle to ride — but I soon became familiar with it. However, the steering was very heavy so it was back to the Internet and Motor-Trike again to order a power steering kit. Then it was a case of dismantling the front end and fitting the power steering. In fact, the conversion meant the front forks were simply raked out a further three degrees or so. The whole job was a most interesting exercise and I have to say both Ros and I are very happy indeed with the result.'

Honda Gold Wing 1500

Overall length: 109 inches

Overall width: 54 inches

Weight: 995 lb

Chassis and suspension: Front half: standard Honda frame
Rear half: 4130 chrome moly ladder bar

Swing arms with progressive shocks

Front forks: 33 degree rake

Differential: altered Ford 2:73 ratio

Final drive: shaft

Front brakes: twin disc

Rear brakes: drum

Compression ratio 9.8:1

Displacement: 1520cc

6 cylinders, horizontally opposed

Colin Tucker

You've got to be totally dedicated to make the grade

For many years the name Colin Tucker was a familiar one in speedway circles, both here in New Zealand and in England, where Colin spent much of his time in the 1970s. A skilled speedway rider who won many championships in his long and colourful career, Auckland-born Colin was also responsible for building six speedway tracks in England. In Colin's case, 'building' literally did mean building — single-handedly, with a hammer and nails and a lot of Kiwi grit and determination. Much has already been written about this larger-than-life character, including the following eulogy to his skill and dedication by Maurie Littlechild, then clerk of the course at the opening of the Crewe Speedway Stadium on 19 May 1969:

'. . . Probably our biggest thanks must go to a lean and likeable New Zealander, Colin Tucker. He has been responsible for the complete installation job and this includes the building of all the inner and outer fences, turnstile buildings, toilets, judges' box, dressing rooms, roadways and, of course, the track and the electrical wiring. Every single nail and screw was put in with his own hands and he has literally worked night and day to get finished in time. He is to be our team captain and he rides in the number seven spot this evening, and to give you

Speedway Bike:
1975 Jawa 500/890 2-Valve
4-stroke: 14:1 compression, single cylinder
Fuel: methanol
Fixed gears
No brakes

Ice Speedway Bike:
1970 Jawa 500/891 2-Valve
4-stroke: 13:1 compression, single cylinder
2-step gearbox
Fuel: methanol
Tyres: rubber 21-inch with 30 mm spikes
Front wheel: left-hand side — 70 spikes, 1 row; centre 17 spikes, 1 row
Back wheel: left-hand side — 38 spikes, 1st row; 38 spikes, 2nd row; centre: 38 spikes, 1 row; right-hand side: 19 spikes, 1 row
No brakes

Little Bike:
1971
Frame: electrical conduit pipe
Back wheel: from fish trolley at Hull docks
Front wheel: from a pram
Wheel centres: 56 cm
No brakes
Motor: 1953 Mosquito Auxiliary Cycle — 38cc
Manufactured by Mosquito Motors Ltd, Liverpool, under licence from Moto Garelli

Speedway Bike:
1966 Hagon/JAP 500 2-Valve
4-stroke: 13.6:1 compression, single cylinder
Fuel: methanol
Fixed gears
No brakes
Frame: Hagon (London)
Motor: JAP (J.A. Priestwick)

Colin Tucker

some idea of this man's dedication to our sport I should tell you that he opted to take part of his wages in the form of a new racing machine, and he will ride it tonight for the first time. Never have I ever wanted to see a man get to the top so much, for if ever anyone deserved it, then that man is Colin Tucker. Give him a special cheer when he appears tonight folks . . . '

Nowadays, the 'retired' Colin runs his own project management company, is a justice of the peace, a marriage celebrant and a gifted amateur photographer. When I chatted to him about his speedway days, however, a gleam came into his eye.

'I entered the speedway game by accident. My main ambition when I left school was to be a dustman. I reckoned that was how you made money! Actually, believe it or not, I was training to be a ballroom dancer when I was bitten by the danger-bug. I had started ballroom dancing just to fill in time between work and night school (I was an apprentice in the building trade). I did quite well dancing and even managed to win a couple of silver medals in ballroom and Latin American. I used to go along with a mate, Peter Smith. Peter went on to become New Zealand champion.

'About the same time, though, I got interested in motorcycles and speedway riding. My mentor in those early days was Maurie Dunn. My interest grew and after two seasons in New Zealand I went over to England and joined the Rockets team in Essex. After that I was over in Germany riding for the New Zealand team with world champion Ivan Mauger, another Kiwi. Then it was back to England, to Crewe and later to Newcastle.'

In spite of an impressive list of achievements on the track, Colin always regarded himself as an average rider, one of the 'lesser lights' in speedway. When asked what it took to be a great speedway rider, Colin was refreshingly honest.

'You have to be a bit silly to even contemplate it. Seriously, though, like any sport, you've got to be totally dedicated to make the grade. That includes your fitness, as well having to be very good mechanically. The secret to being a good speedway rider lies in knowing when to slow down so that you'll live to race another day. I was given that bit of advice from Colin Pratt, the English international rider. If you do it properly, speedway is a safe sport. After all, there are only ever six riders in a race and they are all going the same way.'

Colin Tucker
Selected speedway and motorcycling achievements

1968	1st	Stars of Tomorrow Champion, King's Lynn	England	1975	1st	North Island Championship	New Zealand
1969		Captain Crewe Speedway Team	England	1975	3rd	Auckland Championship	New Zealand
1969		Young Australasian Team	England	1975		New Zealand Test Team	New Zealand
1969	3rd	Cheshire Open Championship	England	1976	3rd	North Island Championship	New Zealand
1969		Knock-out Cup Finalist	England	1976	1st	Auckland Championship	New Zealand
1970		Captain Crewe Speedway Team	England	1976		**World Championship, Australasian Grand Finalist**	New Zealand
1970		Young Australasian Team	England	1976		New Zealand Test Team	New Zealand
1970		New Zealand Test Team	Germany	1977	1st	North Island Championship	New Zealand
1970		England Test Team	New Zealand	1977	1st	Auckland Championship	New Zealand
1971	1st	Yorkshire Best Pairs Champion	England	1978	1st	North Island Championship	New Zealand
1971		England Test Team	New Zealand	1978	3rd	Auckland Championship	New Zealand
1972		Hull Speedway Team Manager	England	1978		**World Championship, Australasian Grand Finalist**	New Zealand
1972		England Test Team Manager	New Zealand	1979	2nd	Auckland Championship	New Zealand
1972		Australasian Test Team Manager	England	1979	2nd	Auckland Championship	New Zealand
1973		Hull Speedway Team Manager	England	1980		New Zealand Test Team Manager	New Zealand
1973		Australasian Team Manager	England	1980	1st	New Zealand Solo Grand Prix Champion	New Zealand
1973	1st	Waikato Open Championship	New Zealand	1981	1st	Auckland Championship	New Zealand
1974		England Test Team Manager	New Zealand				

David Braine

Nobody ever taught me to ride, it just seemed natural

'**I was captivated by motorcycling** from the age of eight or nine when I came across an early Matchless 500 Single in an old shed and I just wanted to know how every part worked. It must be in your blood, because it wasn't until after I bought my first bike when I was fourteen that I discovered my father and uncle had both owned bikes in their youth! Nobody ever taught me to ride, it just seemed natural. Mind you, you need a little more than nature on your side now, due to the power of the modern bikes. I enjoyed buying them, doing them up and selling them to enable me to buy bigger and better bikes. When I was in the fifth form I owned a Triumph 650. Queen Street in Auckland was certainly the place to test your skills on a Friday night; there were more bikes than cars in the seventies, mainly because cars were so expensive.

'My first motorbike, when I was fourteen, was an early 1930 James 175cc. My father gave his consent with the condition that I learned to rebuild the bike from scratch. I did it. Motorcycles saw me through high school, early employment, club weekends, trips around New Zealand and were a constant form of pleasure and relaxation, resulting in long-term friendships.

'A short bikeless spell whilst overseas, followed by family and mortgage, meant that I was unable to indulge my passion for the freedom and excitement of motorcycling again until I was into my early forties.

'Having owned around fourteen bikes over the years I now have the bike of my dreams. The Yamaha V-Max to me is still the ultimate due to its diversity of tremendous power, styling and comfortable ride position. The power it delivers can be infectious, yet it can be ridden comfortably around town. The first V-Max in 1984, with top pro drag racer Pee Wee Gleason at the controls, pulled a nine point six-nine seconds standing quarter mile, still highly respectable even by today's standards. A unique feature of the V-Max is its V boost system. At six thousand revs, butterfly valves progressively open, linking each pair of the four carburettors nestled into the ninety-degree V of the V-Four. Each cylinder then sucks on two carburettors instead of one, the fuel pump doubles its efforts to keep up with demand, and the V-Max begins a headlong rush for the horizon. Before you can say "V-Boost me up, Scotty" you're there. I love character in a motorcycle and the V-Max has character to spare.'

Yamaha V-Max

1198cc

16-valve liquid-cooled

Bore and stroke: 76 x 66 mm

Compression ratio 10.5:1

Carburettor: 35 mm Mikuni W/V-Boost

5-speed transmission

145 hp at 8700 rpm

Final drive: shaft

Norm & Lynda Maddock

We spend every day in the shed and only use the house for sleeping in

When we travelled up to Warkworth to meet Norm and Lynda, we were also introduced to nine cats, Maggie (an elderly, blind dog), a goose and a pet sheep by the name of Penelope. On entering Norm and Lynda's barn our mouths fell open — never had we seen such a collection of motorcycles, parts, bits off old bikes . . . all meticulously labelled and neatly stored. Norm smiled as we admired the old steam radio, still in use and permanently tuned to the Concert Programme. Lynda told us their story:

'Norm was born into a mechanical and technical family of four boys. The family transport was a 1923 Harley-Davidson and side car. As the family grew, the Harley-Davidson was replaced with a new Ford V8, but during the Depression the car had to go and Norm's father went back to a motorcycle, a four-cylinder Henderson with a side-box. In 1939 Norm's eldest brother, Ron, bought a 1937 Rudge, which was taken apart and hidden throughout the family home to prevent it being requisitioned by the army. We still have it.

'Norm has been involved with motorcycles all his life and his particular love is Rudges, a famous make that finished production in 1939. At one stage, he and his brothers all owned Rudges and were well known in the Auckland area.'

The current Rudge, one of the many bikes owned by Norm and Lynda, has an impressive pedigree. It was even used in an advertisement for Rudge Motor Cycles, reproduced here from a copy of the *Motor Cycle* magazine, dated 11 April 1935. Much has already been written about this famous Rudge, now a born-again racing bike. Norm and Lynda bought the 'remains' of the Rudge in 1985 and have meticulously restored it to its original condition. The bike is still regularly raced in classic championships and has competed not only in New Zealand but also in the Isle of Man, Britain and Australia.

'I also come from a mechanical family and was Dad's "little helper" from the age of two. When I was fifteen, Dad bought me an old bike to go to school on. I had to park it under the headmistress's window so that she could keep an eye on it.

I have stayed interested in motorcycles, particularly the mechanical side. When I returned from overseas I went to work for a major motor company. That's where I met Norm, he was my boss. I had arranged to purchase two early Nortons from the South Island and I needed a day off work. The only way my boss would let me take time off was if I agreed to let him buy one of the Nortons. We hadn't known of each

---

1932 Rudge Factory Race Bike

500cc single-cylinder four-stroke

4 semi-radial overhead valves

4-speed close ratio gearbox, foot change

Large bore TT carburettor

Handlebar controlled steering damper

8-inch brakes, front and rear, coupled together

4-gallon petrol tank, twin filler caps

Norm & Lynda Maddock

other's interest in motorcycles until then. The price of the Nortons was two hundred and fifty dollars for the pair — it was a long time ago! — so I agreed to sell one of them to Norm for the same amount. As it turned out, my friend, who was to collect and pay for the two bikes on my behalf, returned empty handed, saying that he did not want to waste my money. After all, no one could possibly want two scruffy old motorcycles with stuffed tyres. He thought he was doing me a good turn. To this day, that particular friend still walks with a pronounced limp.

'Norm and I both share a passionate interest in motorcycling, along with a love of animals, classical music, books and trees. Our idea of a holiday is to go to a motorcycle swap meet in Australia. We spend every day in our shed and only use the house for sleeping in. Our families have long given up hope of us being less one-eyed and more conventional. Given a chance, we would also play with steam engines and early aircraft, but I guess you have to draw the line somewhere.

'I have raced my 1926 AJS in classic races for fourteen years and aim to keep racing it until I'm at least ninety!'

1932 Rudge Factory Race Bike
As it appeared in a 1935 issue of Motor Cycle *magazine*

Judy de Leeuwe

I loved all the chrome work and the sound the engine made

Currently working as general manager for Pacey Trucks, Judy has had a lifelong interest in the automotive world.

'I have always been interested in motor vehicles, including motorcycles, cars and trucks. The engineering and sheer speed of motor vehicles has always enthralled me. As a toddler, I had toy cars and motorbikes and as a young child, while travelling in the family car, could identify cars and bikes we passed. As I grew up I read the automotive section in the paper and was able to tell my parents the specs of these vehicles — top speed, torque, engine size and so on. I was fortunate that my interest in motor vehicles did not faze my parents; in fact, they even encouraged me.

'When I was thirteen I learned to ride my boyfriend's trail bike, a Suzuki TS185. The moment I turned fifteen I had my car licence and in order to get my bike licence I made a deal with my parents that I would go through the then "Coca Cola Riding School". I'm really glad I did it. It meant that I learnt to ride defensively and enabled me to go from a provisional to a full licence a lot quicker. Then, of course, I purchased my first bike. It was a Suzuki TS250 trail bike which I used for riding to school and university. Lack of finance meant that I couldn't buy a more powerful bike, but the trail bike at least *looked* bigger than a road bike!

'At eighteen I started work at Coleman Suzuki, eventually becoming parts manager. Working in a bike shop gave me the perfect opportunity to change bikes, so, at eighteen, I fell for a Honda CB750 K2 which had just been traded in. It had had only one owner and was exceptionally tidy and original, except for an after-market exhaust system, which I changed immediately. Here was a big bike with great lines. I loved all the chrome work and the sound the engine made. It was a real classic. I still have the bike today, it has never lost its appeal.

'I also worked as a race mechanic for the late Roger Freeth and other motorcycle racers, so I got to ride their race bikes. Roger didn't ride much on the road, he thought it was a bit unsafe with all the cars out there! However, I gladly accepted the responsibility of running the engines in on the road before they were transplanted to the McIntosh race frames that he used.

'I have ridden many off-road bikes for weekend fun, the most exciting being a Suzuki RM465 Z — the first year of the single-shock Suzukis. I also took up rally navigating and competed as a driver in rally sprints.

'My work moved into both cars and trucks so it only seemed natural to get my heavy truck and trailer licence. I still work in the motor industry and ride my Honda. I still love both, even after twenty years! My bike has become such a part of me that I'll never sell it. I don't see why I shouldn't ride it for at least the next twenty years.'

1973 Honda CB750 K2

Engine: 736cc OHC 4-cylinder

Transverse in-line 4-stroke

Aluminium alloy

Air-cooled

Bore and stroke: 61 x 63 mm

Compression: 9:1

Carburettors: four 28 mm piston valve

Starting: electric push-button or kick

Transmission: 5-speed

Dimensions: 2160 x 870 x 1170 mm

Tank capacity: 17 litres

Weight: 218 kg

Alister Stevens

I'll still be riding my bike when I'm really old

Based in Invercargill, Alister Stevens has been a professional firefighter for the past 23 years. As a firefighter facing the grim reality of disasters and road accidents as part of his job, Alister is very aware of the dangers involved in motorcycling. However, a self-confessed 'petrolhead', Alister loves anything with an engine and wheels.

'You can't help but be aware of the danger. My partner, Jo, is a former ambulance woman and I suppose, between us, we've seen a lot of things that most people would rather not think about. From a very young age I have always had a love of engines and horsepower and a broad interest in most kinds of vehicles, but particularly in motorcycles. In the last seven years I have owned an XZ400 Yamaha, an FZR600 Yamaha Genesis, a 95 Harley-Davidson DWG and in March last year I purchased a brand new Triumph Daytona 955i, which I still own.

'While I would still like to ride a tourer of some kind, the petrolhead side of me still makes me lean over on a sports bike at this stage. The Triumph has everything I like in a bike — the styling, the reliability, and an awesome power-to-weight ratio. It handles and brakes very well and I find it comfortable enough on long rides. The bike feels very safe at high speed, which I confess to having done in small bursts from time to time. Jo has reminded me on a few occasions now that, unlike the fire appliance, the bike hasn't got flashing lights and a siren to warn people that I'm coming!

'I love riding around the South Island where the scenery is just great. The West Coast on a fine day is fantastic, but I enjoy riding even on a wet, cold day. As long as you've got the right riding gear and wet weather gear, it really isn't a problem, you just have to get out there.

'I ride with a really good bunch of workmates and friends and we attend quite a few rallies each year. I'm forty-three now and I see people of all ages at the rallies, from young to very old. I would like to think that I'll still be riding my bike when I'm really old, too. I just can't imagine ever giving it up.'

1999 Triumph Daytona 955i

Engine: in-line 3-cylinder fuel-injected

4-stroke

128 hp

Water-cooled

Digital inductive ignition

On-board computer management system

Runs on 96 octane gas

Fuel tank: 18-litre

Gearbox: 6-speed unit with wet, multi-plate clutch system

Dry weight: 198 kg

Front brakes: twin disc

Rear brakes: single disc

Modifications: high-rise carbon fibre muffler and exhaust

Vince Hyde

I can still hear Dad saying 'No bikes, boy, you'll kill yourself'

Vince was 38 when he got his first bike and he could still hear his father's stern words ringing in his ears:

'Oh yes, believe me, I can still hear Dad saying "No bikes, boy, you'll kill yourself!" You get to the stage, though, when you just have to follow your heart's desire. I got my licence on a Honda 50 back in 1976. At the time I already had my heavy trade, heavy trailer and bus licences. The testing officer asked me what bike I was riding. When I told him it was a Honda 50 he looked at me and said, 'You at your age and a bike that size? You won't get into trouble.' Believe it or not he then wrote out the licence without me answering any questions or doing the practical test. I don't think that would happen nowadays. Mind you, it was in Kaeo in the far North.

'Did you notice the number plate on my bike? It's "I'm over 50!" When you reach fifty in the Ulysses Club you get to become a senior member. You only have to be forty to be a junior member. It's a well-known fact that the function of the juniors is to help the seniors on and off their bikes.'

Married to Raewyn for 28 years and with their two sons now aged 23 and 25, Vince reckons that the 'empty nest' syndrome fuelled his passion for motorcycling. He and Raewyn now have the time and the freedom to enjoy exploring the highways and byways of New Zealand on their Honda Gold Wing.

'We have toured the South Island three times now. We both enjoy music, particularly piano and guitar music. There's nothing nicer than cruising through a valley with the cruise control set to about ninety-five kilometres per hour and Vivaldi playing on the stereo. If we want to talk to each other we have an intercom on the Gold Wing with 'voice activated mute' — the music automatically quietens down when we speak.

'We really enjoy doing charity runs, too. In March each year we do the Cambridge to Hamilton run. The Air Force bring a bus load of children suffering from cancer down from the Waikato Hospital. Members of the Ulysses Club then take the children back to the Cloudlands Show Grounds. The Auckland branch of the Ulysses Club also raised ten thousand dollars from selling T-shirts and badges for the Westpac Helicopter Trust. It's very rewarding to be part of that sort of thing.'

1996 Honda Gold Wing
1500cc engine
6-cylinder

Des Trubshoe

Adventure riding is great as I can enjoy myself without speeding

Des Trubshoe — Trubbie to his friends — has certainly led a very active life. Now 58, he first started riding motorcycles in 1956. He has been a show jumper, a rodeo rider, a water skier, a diver and for some twelve years he was well known on the saloon car racing circuit.

'My first bike was a 1952 Tiger 100, which I owned for about a year. It was a terrible bike. The motor seemed to last about the same length of time as a pair of tyres. My second bike was a 1956 Gold Flash, which seemed better as the motor lasted for two sets of tyres. Various other bikes followed and then in 1983 I got my first big capacity bike, a brand new XV1000. I travelled about fifty thousand kilometres on that machine. When I traded it in for a 1988 FJ1200 I lost my licence within six months for speeding. I had to part with the bike altogether in 1991 to pay off some debts.

'In 1993 — several bikes later — I bought my first ST1100. I also started adventure riding. En route to my first South Island BMW safari, I towed an XR400 behind my ST1100 on a small trailer, all the way from Whangarei to Picton. I did the adventure ride, then toured the South Island on the ST with my wife, Valerie.

'Before she met me, Val had never been on a bike. She had never slept in a tent either. After only one date I asked her if she fancied a trip to the Far North adventure ride. She didn't know what she was letting herself in for. Her first ride turned out to be three hundred kilometres and just a bit hair-raising. At one point we were riding on top of a ridge. The track was only a metre wide, with the sea on either side. 'What a neat view,' I said. Val couldn't comment, she had her eyes shut. She still married me, though. The next year, while touring the South Island — on our honeymoon — I traded the ST1100 for a brand new Honda Gold Wing. I had it for nine months and did twenty-one thousand kilometres on it . . . but I hated it. It was just not me. I ended up trading it back in for another new ST.

'I also added a Honda VFR800 to my bike collection, so now I've got everything covered. For touring with Val I use the ST1100, for rallies in the winter and other rides that I do on my own, I use the VFR800 and, of course, I've got the Suzuki DR250 for adventure rides.

'I had some heart trouble back in 1996, so they gave me a titanium implant. The doctors told me not to drive, but they didn't tell me not to ride my bike. Two weeks after the operation I rode to Russell and Whangarei, then a week later I was at the Far North rally.

'I usually manage to do about thirty thousand kilometres a year in total. Valerie enjoys motorcycling with me now, but she doesn't like cold weather, so in winter it's a case of going it alone. I do the Cold Kiwi, the Frozen Pines and other cold rides on my own on the VFR800. I prefer to do adventure rides on my own too. That way I don't have to worry about hurting Val if I fall. Adventure riding is great as I can enjoy myself without speeding. On the metal, a hundred kilometres an hour is quite fast enough.'

Suzuki DR250

Engine size: 248cc

Fuel capacity: 10 litres

Starting system: electric

Final drive: chain drive

Dry weight: 113 kg

Tyre size: 450 x 18 inches rear, 21 inches front

Trevor Hall

Nowadays I find I'm more a connoisseur of the finer machines

The sky is the limit for this enterprising Kiwi — in the back of the photograph of Trevor with his gourmet collection of motorcycles, rests his own hand-built aeroplane.

'I was a schoolboy of fourteen in the 1970s when I got my first Pommie bike, a 1954 Norton ES2. As the years went past I owned numerous other makes and models — Matchless, BSA, Triumph, AJS, Cossack, Ariel, Panther, Harley-Davidson and Guzzi — to name but a few. I did all my own repairs and maintenance, learning from my mistakes, from books and from more experienced motorcyclists.

'I've owned my Vincent Black Shadow for sixteen years now. I rode it to my wedding and the key here is that I rode it home again and I didn't have to sell it. You have to have an understanding wife to have a motorcycle collection. Vincents are great bikes. As you can see in the photograph, the Black Shadow has the initials HRD on the side. These initials stood for Harold Ronald Davies, the designer. However, post-1950 models were manufactured without the initials because too many people were confusing the bikes with Harley-Davidsons. Mine is a 1949 model, I did up the motor when I first bought it in 1984 and I haven't had to do much at all to it since. It's the sports version of the Vincent Rapide touring model. It has a cruising speed of about a hundred miles per hour and a top speed of about a hundred and thirty, not bad at all for a 1949 motorcycle! Vincents used to be the fastest standard motorcycles in the world. They gained a reputation for breaking all kinds of world records. I believe one record has yet to be broken, namely the speed record for a motorcycle with sidecar, set in 1955 with a speed of one hundred and sixty-five point eight miles per hour. Now there's a challenge for you . . .

'In recent years I have gone into business and opened a motorcycle shop here in Te Awamutu, which caters for all British, American and European motorcycles. I service and repair anything from BSA C10s right through to Harleys, BMWs and Guzzis.

'With demand of business, family and my recent hobby of building a plane and flying, nowadays I find I'm more a connoisseur of the finer machines. I have what I like to think of as a collection of thoroughbreds and I savour the times that I can get out and enjoy them.'

Motorcycles in photograph from left to right:

BSA 750cc

HRD Vincent Black Shadow

Cruising speed: 100 mph

Top speed: 130 mph

Brake system unique to Vincent: four brake units: two at front, two at rear

1996 Triumph Daytona

1200cc

140 hp

Vincent Number 232

Norvin Racing Bike

1000cc

Motor manufactured in 1947

Frame manufactured circa 1958

Forks/front wheel: 1962 Norton Manx

Wayne & Dale Painter

I shall always ride, either on my own or as a pillion passenger

'**Wayne and I have been married** now for thirty years, not a bad achievement. We were together for six years before that, so I suppose we knew what we were in for. Wayne rode motorcycles as a young man but, of course, marriage and kids took over and for some reason we were more interested in four-wheeled transport in the early days. We enjoyed car trials, rallies, club racing, you know the sort of thing. In 1991, though, Wayne bought a 650 Suzuki Savage with a pillion seat resembling a small vinyl-covered brick. He only had it for thirteen days, but by then the damage was done, it was motorcycles all the way. A succession of bikes followed: three BMWs, a Kawasaki Voyager and a Kawasaki GPZ1100. In late 1997 Wayne bought his 1500cc Honda Valkyrie. After three trips around the South Island on pillion I started to think that it might be fun to ride myself. I had never ridden before, you realise, not even a push-bike. However, my fiftieth birthday was looming large and a new goal was needed. I decided that I would aim to have my motorcycle licence before I turned the big five-o! I started to learn on a 125 Suzuki, in 1996 I bought a new Kawasaki ZZR250 and on Valentine's Day 1997 Wayne bought me my new Honda VFR750.

'My bike is called "Grandma's Revenge" because just before I bought my first bike my son anounced that I was to become a grandmother. I decided that after years of worrying about what the kids were up to it was time they started worrying about me.

'Wayne and I joined the Ulysses Club in 1991 and for the last four years Wayne has been the co-ordinator for the Auckland branch. For me, having learned to ride later in life, each stage of riding, from getting my licence to overcoming hurdles (it took me a while to learn how to get in and out of our driveway on the bike) to accomplishing rides in varying weather conditions, has given me a tremendous sense of achievement that I do not think I could get in any other way. Our big plan now is to take our bikes to Australia for an extended tour.

'I have now been involved with motor-cycling for eight years and just cannot imagine being without a bike. I shall always ride, either on my own or as a pillion passenger. When Wayne and I are no longer able to hold up two wheels we will probably end up on a pair of trikes.'

Dales bike:
Honda VFR750

Engine size: 748cc

Bore and stroke: 70.0 x 48.6 mm

Compression ratio: 11.0:1

Fuel tank capacity: 21 litres

Dry weight: 210 kg

Overall length: 2100 mm

Overall width: 720 mm

Overall height: 1185 mm

Wayne's bike:
Honda Valkyrie

Engine size: 1520cc

Bore and stroke: 71 x 64 mm

Compression ratio: 9.8:1

Fuel tank capacity: 20 litres

Dry weight: 309 kg

Overall length: 2530 mm

Overall width: 980 mm

Overall height: 1185 mm

Peter Bryant

My first real restoration project was a 1937 Empire Star

'**I've always regretted** the introduction of helmets by compulsion. It was hard enough to cut a dash around Devonport on an L.E. Velocette without having a pudding basin strapped to your head.'

English-born Peter Bryant has lived in New Zealand since the age of sixteen. With an irrepressible sense of humour, Peter has some hilarious tales to tell about his experiences as a motorcyclist.

'I did my first major tour on a 125 Vespa in 1965: Auckland to Wellington, the ferry to Picton, then Bluff, Invercargill, Milford Sound, Haast Pass, Picton and return. My arse took a year to recover. The high point came when I ran out of gas in Reefton. I had four shillings and sixpence to get back to Auckland. The gas station was closed — yeah, *the* gas station! I was told the proprietor of the gas station was in the pub and that he would open up for me and my four and six-worth of petrol. I was eighteen years old, I had never been in a pub before, especially a miners' pub (as in coal miners). Imagine the long bar, the mirrors and the silence "for inspection purposes".

'"What d'yer want, lad?" said a voice, not unkindly.

'"Ah, I er need some petrol . . ."

'"Jeez, boy, the grog's not that bad," came the gruff voice. There followed laughter and then another voice spoke from behind a cloud of Craven A. "Be there in a minute, boy." I stood, like sixpence, waiting. The bartender eyed my cork helmet. "What sort of bike are you on, lad?" he asked.

'"Er . . . that," I replied as I pointed out of the window.

'"Kerrrrist, what is it? Hey, fellas, come and look at this." The whole bar-full trooped over and looked. There was stunned silence. Then, "Jeez, boy, the lumps of road metal on the Pass are bigger than your wheels!" And he was right.

'"Would you like a beer, lad?" the barman asked. I was getting to like this bloke. He called me "lad" not "boy" and offered me alcohol. "Sorry," I stammered, "I can't afford it, I've only got four and six and that's for petrol."

'He looked puzzled. "Where ya heading?"

'"Back to Auckland," I replied.

'"Ya what? On four and bloody six? Bloody Auckland? On that? Right, you lot, SHURRUP!" The bar fell quiet. "Laddy is going to Auckland. On four and bloody six. Okay . . . Divvy up."

'I felt about two foot tall, which wasn't bad

1954 Vincent

499cc

Push rod operated

AMAL carburettor

4-speed Burman gearbox

1930s Dusting sidecar

Pivot-action rear spring hydraulically dampened suspension

Peter Bryant

going considering I was six foot three and built like a streak of weasel pee. Scarred hands delved into pockets and coal-blue veined arms pushed a growing heap of change to my end of the counter — a small mountain of tanners, bobs, two bobs, half crowns, threepenny bits and copper — a small fortune.

'"Would you like that beer now, lad?" asked the barman. I didn't reply. I couldn't even see . . .

'Two weeks later the Reefton Pub burned to the ground. Ever since I have regretted not being able to send my thanks to those men at that pub. *And* four and bloody six.

'Time passed by — girls (at least the ones who would go out with me) wouldn't be seen dead on a bike. When you're full of testosterone something has to give. In my case Mum and Dad died in the space of a year and I was cast adrift with a small legacy from Dad. I bought a sports car (a Spitfire) and then an MGB, then a 240 Datsun. I raced 'em, rallied 'em and rogered 'em (the last in my wet dreams). It turned out that most of the lasses weren't at all averse to snuggling up on a pillion — they'd just objected to nipple-pink and lime-green Italian two-strokes!

'In the late 1960s and early 1970s British bikes were mostly basket cases. Harleys were for *old* people and the Japanese were producing usable, quick, reliable and sanitary vehicles. I had Suzukis, Kawasakis, Hondas and Yamahas. I also fettled and rode my brother's bikes: Triumphs, Nortons, AJSs, BSAs, Royal Enfield Vincents, Velocettes and an SS80 Brough. So I never *owned* a British bike. Yet there was seldom a time when there wasn't one in various stages of undress in one corner of the garage. I could never afford an old bike (I understand they call them "Vintage" or "Classics" now) as a hobby and work required reliability, just as two kids required a sidecar. Sixteen years on and I've still got the same chair and bike — a Yamaha 750 Triple — and I've put three hundred and fifty thousand kilometres on it.

'My first real restoration project was a 1937 Empire Star. I couldn't source a carburettor anywhere in the English-speaking world. I saw Len Perry at his Red Shed on the Great South Road in Auckland. "Scarce as hens' teeth, those," said Len. "Do you want a new one or a used one?" He turned. He had one in each hand.

'After a quarter of a century of teaching I retired with my partner to our quarter acre of paradise in Te Awamutu. I now have two Yamaha Triples, a leaky 3TA (borrowed), two sidecars and "Vince". Vince has been a bit sulky in the piston area since he came to us from Nelson. The previous owners, Don Harris and Dr Miles Hursthouse, had loved and cared for him, especially Miles, who looked after him for twenty-five years and fitted the sidecar. We learned from Trevor Hall of Te Awamutu that Vince was languishing and when we found out the price we understood why. Still, you get to fifty-something, you've got no debts (well, not many anyway), you've never owned a British bike, your mates and relations have a dozen and you suddenly realise you'll be riding a Honda in heaven if you don't do something — and quickly. So Vince made the big crossing over Raukawa Moana to Te Ika a Maui and promptly spat the electrical and ignition systems before becoming externally lubricated due to being "piston broke".

'Words have been spoken, entrails cast and the runes consulted. In other words, Trevor Hall and the Vincent Owners Club have joined to heal the wounds of time. Soon, Vince will be once again scaring the Waikato cows with his staccato bark, and as for me, I'll be a lot poorer, but one hell of a lot happier, as I head off into the sunset.'

| 1937 Empire Star

Peggy O'Neal
Vespas don't die, you've got to kill them

'In 1993 I saw a lot of these scooters around and I just fell in love with them. They had my name on them — well, in Italian anyway, "Piaggio".' (Piaggio isn't Italian for Peggy, but Peggy reckons if she tells people often enough they'll believe it.) 'I made inquiries and decided to purchase one that December, but I wanted a red one. I had to wait for the next shipment.

'My red Vespa duly arrived and all the paperwork was done by March seventeenth. With a name like mine, Saint Patrick's Day seemed very fitting. I started travelling to Whangarei, Matapouri and back. My first trip took three days — well, I had three days to do it in. It was quite a big adventure, a hundred and ninety kilometres on a little Vespa.

'From that, of course, it was on to bigger and longer adventures. Next, I thought I'd go round East Cape. After all, it was only three hundred and fourteen kilometres.'

'Six months after purchasing my scooter I joined the Ulysses Club, a group of very like-minded people. I have had many a good rally with Ulysses, meeting people from Kaitaia to Invercargill, where the second AGM in my time with the club was held. Two years later I was off to Dunedin, then Wanganui via Nelson and Napier. "Ooops, I'm off" seems to have stuck with me.

'My last "Oops, I'm off" nearly ended in disaster. I was coming down the north side of East Cape when a great amount of air took off — from my rear wheel. I had picked up a pop rivet as I went round a corner. I managed the corner and got some control. I said to myself, "We'll land there" looking at a nice grassy drain. Well, I guess I either hit a rock or put the front brake on. Whatever I did, the scooter nose-dived and I went flying over the top. Apparently I looked quite good from my riding mate's point of view. I'm not sure if I landed on my head or not as my leg hurt (a lot) and my head (not as much), but my helmet was never to be used again. The cracks were visible. As you might imagine, the next seventy kilometres to our destination were rather slow. It's a good job the Vespa carried a spare tyre.

'I never anticipated the great love and enjoyment I would get from my Vespa. I commute on it ten kilometres daily and I just love it. When touring I am able to see so much more of the scenery than faster bikes. I have travelled with faster riders who have slowed down to ride with me and have heard favourable comments as to how much they enjoyed the ride. I also love riding on my own and meeting up with people at fuel stops and at my destination.

'Roads I have liked, loved or just conquered include the Gentle Annie, East Cape, the Paraparas, Collingwood/Farewell Spit, Rimutakas, Waipu to Wellsford via Mangawhai, and my all-time favourite Wellsford/Helensville — the Kaipara view is just wonderful. Come to think of it, I haven't come across a road that I really hate — just as well really.

'Buying a scooter is the best lifestyle choice I have made. The bruises, the aches and pains have certainly been worth it. I have met a wealth of nice people the length and breadth of New Zealand. Vespas don't die, you've got to kill them.'

1994 Piaggio Vespa 200cc Scooter

Colin Ottaway

The bike went through a series of mishaps over the years

Born in Auckland in the late 1940s, Colin is the first to admit that he was not destined to set the world alight with his academic abilities.

'I attended school mainly to eat my lunch until the fourth form when I decided that if I was ever going to succeed in life as a bad arse biker then I would, of course, need a bike . . . and this wasn't going to happen on earnings from a paper round. Having already learned to ride on an older mate's 650 Bathtub Triumph Thunderbird it was suddenly "Goodbye School" and "Hello Unskilled Labourer".

'Shortly after it was a matter of a trip to Bill Russell's bike shop in Mount Eden Road and I was the proud owner of a 1954 Spring Hub Triumph Speed Twin for the goodly sum of one hundred pounds. This bike was immaculate, painted black and a deep silvery green. It looked really smart until I introduced it to beer and found that it couldn't even make its way home after a few drinks. It used to fall down and go to sleep at the first opportunity! The bike went through a succession of mishaps over the years — wet roads, white lines, cars turning out of side streets, parked cars, telegraph poles, bus shelters, to name but a few.

'I wonder if some kindly old bloke has found my old bike and restored it to its former glory. It would be nice to think someone is taking it out on Sundays for a back-breaking ride around the neighbourhood then bringing it home, polishing it and putting it back in the shed on its own carpet with a sheet over it. I hope it has got its own little drip tray, too.

'The old ST was followed by a number of other British bikes and then came the farm bikes, trail bikes, motocross bikes and, in the late eighties, another road bike, a 1982 Honda CB750 C. Shortly after came my introduction to the Ulysses Club, of which I became member number two-nine-six and heavily involved in the Tauranga branch.

'In 1990 I got my first *new* bike, a Kawasaki Vulcan 1500, to be followed by a GPZ900 Ninja, an 800 Vulcan and then my present bike, a 1997 Vulcan 1500 Classic. I am currently the co-ordinator for the Waihi Thames Valley Branch of the Ulysses Club of New Zealand.'

Christine, Colin's wife of three years and partner of seven, also shares Colin's passion for motorcycling. Gaining her licence in 1987 on her Suzuki NZ250, Christine then went on to own a black Suzuki GSXR250, a silver Honda CMX 450 Rebel and now she is the proud owner of a 1999 Suzuki VS800 Intruder ('Lollipop').

'There are days when my garden is crying out for attention and I just want to potter in it,' she says, ' but being married to an avid biker means the highway comes first, so it's a case of going for a ride or staying home on my own again.'

Kawasaki Vulcan 1500 Classic

Engine: 4-stroke, liquid-cooled V-Twin

Bore and stroke: 102 x 90 mm

Compression ratio: 8.6:1

Valve system: SOHC, 8 valves

Carburation: Keihin CVK 40

Ignition: digital

Transmission: 4-speed with positive neutral finder

Fuel capacity: 16 litres

Dry weight: 292 kg

Marcus Hartmann

I have owned bikes from both ends of the power spectrum

Born in Switzerland in 1945, Marcus Hartmann has lived in New Zealand for over 30 years. He has managed to hang on to his accent, but this boy is a real Kiwi motorcycle enthusiast.

'In Switzerland a driver's licence can only be acquired at eighteen years of age, but the attitude to driving is not necessarily different, you get the same hooligans everywhere. I learned to ride on my father's Lambretta Scooter, but soon had my own bike, a 50cc Zuendapp Sportsbike. I well remember my first long tour — a two and a half thousand kilometre trip from Switzerland to the North Sea in Belgium. With a top speed of seventy kilometres per hour the trip took me twenty-one hours one way in one stretch. After that, I had a succession of bikes, mostly two-strokes, before I gradually built up to the big one.

'After a stint in the army, I worked in Switzerland and toured parts of Europe for another four years, my main form of transport being, of course, my motorcycle. When I immigrated to these lovely shores in 1969 I managed to get a job at the Hermitage Hotel at Mount Cook. Sadly I was without a bike for some six years, but when I moved to Auckland I was able to buy my first New Zealand motorcycle. I needed some cheap transport and a motorcycle was the only way to go.

'In 1995 I joined the Ulysses Motorcycle Club in Auckland and started some serious touring of this wonderful country. I'm looking forward to many more kilometres of motorcycling and discovery on these beautiful shores.

'Over the years I have owned many bikes and have loved each one for its own special character. I have owned bikes from both ends of the power spectrum. From the Velosolex (which on occasions I could probably have overtaken on foot!) to my current love, the Yamaha V-Max — even Superman would have trouble keeping up with this machine! Exhilarating.'

Yamaha V-Max

1198cc

16-valve, liquid-cooled

Bore and stroke: 76 x 66 mm

Compression ratio: 10.5:1

Carburettor: 35 mm Mikuni W/V-Boost

5-speed transmission

145 hp at 8700 rpm

Final drive: shaft

Dave & Carol Yells
I spent more time pushing the Francis Barnett than riding it

It would seem that the love of motorcycling is almost hereditary. Carol holds her great-uncle responsible . . . and her father . . . and then, of course, there was her brother . . . she didn't stand a chance.

'I grew up with a family history of motorcycles. My great-uncle was Lloyd Dixon, winner of both the Junior and Senior Waiheke TT in 1938. My own first ride on a motorcycle was as a toddler on my father's 1942 Indian, his regular transport at the time. My brother rode motocross for several years in the seventies and eighties and my dad was a senior steward. I didn't stand a chance really, I *had* to love motorcycles. Of course, when I married Dave, road bikes had to go by the board for a while. We had to make do with farm bikes. But the passion for motorcycles was always there.

'When we moved to the Karangahake Gorge in the mid eighties, the motorcycles passing by on State Highway 2 on the weekends were just too much. We had to go out and buy one! We bought our first motorcycle together — a 1987 Suzuki GS1100 G — from the late Brian Barnsley of Hamilton Motorcycles. It was Brian who signed us up as members of the Ulysses Club. We decided the best way to meet other members was to go to a few rallies. The first one was at Kelly Park, north of Auckland. We loaded up and headed off, not knowing what we would find when we got there. All went well until, with just a couple of corners to go, we came to a T intersection. No signs. I said "right" and Dave said "left". We went left. As soon as we had turned the corner it was obvious that we should have turned right. Dave pulled over to the side . . . a bit too close to the water table. His foot slid and we were in a foot or so of deep, loose metal — before we knew it we had started to lose vertical hold. To avoid ending up in a heap at the bottom Dave rode the bike right the way down. We sat laughing in relief as several other riders passed by wondering what the heck we were up to.

Dave started riding motorcycles 'of necessity' back in England in 1953. He hasn't looked back.

'My first bike was a 1934 Frances Barnett Falcon 38, quickly followed by a 1933 Sunbeam 350cc Model 8. Unfortunately I spent more time pushing the Frances Barnett than riding it. Then came a 1953 Frances Barnett Scrambler, which I used as regular transport.

'In 1956 I arrived on the shores of New Zealand as a Ten Pound Pom. I started motorcycling here on a 1954 500cc Velocette MSS, travelling from Katikati to Papakura. I remember it was colder on the Hauraki Plains that winter than it was when I was riding in the snow the previous winter in the UK.

'In 1960 I bought a 1951 Matchless 500, which I converted for use in scrambling competitions in and around Whakatane. After Carol and I bought the Suzuki, we purchased a 1983 Yamaha Venture and we're now the proud owners of a 1997 Honda Valkyrie Tourer. The trike is the latest addition to our "fleet". It means a new riding style and more fun in the future.'

1997 Honda Valkyrie GL 1500 CT

1500cc liquid-cooled engine

6-cylinder motor

Belt-driven overhead cam shafts

Produces 100 hp at 5800 rpm

Doug Kay

For my eightieth birthday I've ordered myself a flame-orange Buell

'**I'm treating myself** to a new bike soon,' chuckles Doug. 'For my eightieth birthday I've ordered myself a flame-orange Buell.

'I started work in March 1937 and after a few months of paying bus fares (eight pence per day) I decided a motorcycle was cheaper transport so I bought a 1929, 500cc AJS for ten pounds. When the Second World War started I had graduated to a 1939, 500cc Calthorpe, which I used for racing on the beach and grass track meetings.

'I was in the right age bracket and so was called up for army duty. At my interview I asked to be a dispatch rider. I received notice to enter Waiouru Camp in December 1939 and was told to bring the motorbike. New Zealand was not prepared for war. The army had no motorbikes of its own so fourteen of us formed a Dispatch Riders Platoon with our own bikes. Safety gear was unheard of, no one bothered with helmets or boots. We rode during the day and at night (no lights allowed) and at the end of training in May 1940 we were sent back to civilian life to await a call for overseas service.

'I could get no guarantee that I could be a dispatch rider so I applied to the RNZAF as an engineer. I had already been declined as a pilot because of my eyesight. I had enough credentials to be accepted as an engineer and was eventually called up in September 1941. Once the six months' training was over I was posted to a station and it was back to motorcycles. I am certain I did more riding in the air force than I would have done in the army. I had plenty of petrol and I usually had two bikes — a good one and one to hack around. I had three years in Nelson and the aerodrome was near to Tahuna Beach. I spent many hours roaring up and down that beach. I went to Motueha at least once a week and always made sure that I did the thirty mile run in thirty minutes. There was virtually no other traffic, of course, and I used my factory OK Supreme. This bike had been imported to New Zealand to try for the 500cc speed record. It broke the record in Christchurch in 1939, ridden by Llew Evans. The average speed both ways over a flying mile was a hundred and fourteen point five miles per hour!

'After marriage in late 1949 I was without a bike for a short period, but then the desire returned. Since then I have had about thirty bikes — from 250cc two-strokes up to the larger bike I have today. One bike I had was a Yamaha FZ600. When the new FZRs came out I bought one. At that time I had a Harley Davidson 1200cc Sportster and a Yamaha TW 250cc Trail Bike. I kept the FZR until I bought a 1995 Bimota SB6. This was the fastest production bike in the world. I still have this bike, as well as a 1996 Bimota Mantra with a Ducati 904cc engine. I also have a 1999 Buell X1, the one in the photograph. The engine on the Buell started as a 1203cc Harley-Davidson but has Erik Buell's own cylinder heads, larger valves, cams, fuel injection and so on. The Buells are being raced successfully in the USA and Australia and already hold ten world records. I can't forsee how long I will be riding my Buell. Until my death — I hope.'

1999 Buell X1

2-cylinder

Air-cooled, 4-stroke, 45-degree V-Twin

Bore and stroke: 88.8 x 96.8 mm.

Piston displacement: 1203cc

Compression ratio: 10:1

101 hp at 6000 rpm

Fuel tank capacity: 17.41 litres

Chris Parker

The first motorcycle I ever owned was a Royal Enfield and sidecar

Over the years, Chris has spent an awful lot of time and money on restoring old bikes. His wife, Glenis, has perfected the art of 'tit-for-tat' spending.

'When we first got married I already had a house and was well settled in. However, one of the first things Glenis did was to suggest that I remove the 1947 Royal Enfield that I was restoring from the kauri table in the bedroom and put it in the garage! I became interested in motorcycles during the 1970s after my uncle, Roland Partridge, took me flat out along a beach in the sidecar of his Velocette. I was hooked and vowed to get one. I've owned many bikes since then. If I go out and buy another motorcycle, or get expensive work done, Glenis spends money too. My first motorcycle purchase after we got married led to Glenis going out and buying a three-hundred-dollar bedspread. Over the years Glenis has built up a great china collection and done a few trips thanks to my motorcycles. We moved out to the country to get more room for my bikes. We have a huge barn, which is now full.

'The first motorcycle I ever owned was a Royal Enfield and sidecar. I'd never ridden a bike before, let alone one with a sidecar. When I finally figured out how to get it going I learned very quickly that leaning into the corner doesn't work. I went straight across the road, up the gutter and onto the footpath, narrowly missing a power pole.

'In 1988 a friend and I decided to go to England and bring back a vintage motorcycle each. I left my wife at home with our two small children — I still don't know how I got away with it. We went to see a chap who had about two hundred bikes, all for sale. Like kids in a candy shop, we couldn't believe our eyes. We ended up with three bikes — a 1931 Sunbeam 500, a 1947 Velocette 350 KSS and a 1955 Royal Enfield 350 Trials Bike.

'Over the years I've sent and received parts for bikes to and from Finland, Sweden, Latvia, Germany, England, Scotland, Italy, USA, Canada, Australia and South Africa. And just think — all these people would be happy to see me if I arrived on their doorstep simply because I'm a motorcycle enthusiast.'

Chris Parker has restored many motorcycles over the years, two of which are photographed here. Chris himself describes his much-loved 'Peashooter' and his 1929 Harley-Davidson.

1925 Harley-Davidson Peashooter 25 'S'

350cc (21 cubic inch) single cylinder

OHV, 2 valves per cylinder

Tyres:
28 X 21/4 beaded edge run at 80 PSI

Forks:
special Harley-Davidson racing

Steel flywheels

Roller tappets

Bosch magneto

Magnesium alloy piston

Fuel:
75% wood alcohol, 25% benzole

Maximum rpm 7000

Carburettor:
Schebler rotary racing

Single speed, no clutch

Chris Parker

1925 Harley-Davidson Peashooter 25 'S'

'The Harley-Davidson 350 Single in the photograph is a pre-production dirt track racer from 1925. This is one of very few made by the factory and loaned out to Harley-Davidson agents in countries where they hoped to compete against English motorcycles. Brought to New Zealand in 1929 by Lionel Van Praag (who became the first world speedway champion in 1936) it's a pure circuit racer with no brakes, clutch or gears, and was designed for a rolling start. I purchased it as an engineless frame. Harley-Davidson USA provided original photographs and with Ken Campbell's framework and my searching for parts and assembly I'm glad to say it is now back to its former glory. The single speed racing models were originally called 'Peashooters' due to their short exhaust pipes making a noise like a peashooter. Only about ten of this particular model were ever made.'

1929 Harley-Davidson 7/9 'J' Twin Cylinder

'The 1929 Harley-Davidson 7/9 was the last restoration by Geoff Hockley of Christchurch. Geoff was the driving force behind motorcycles in the New Zealand Vintage Car Club and he wrote many articles on old motorcycles and motorcycling. The bike was "shovelled" off the tray of a truck and Geoff restored it for the 1972 International Rally. Geoff gave up motorcycling in 1975 and sold the bike to someone in Nelson. I swapped a 1923 Harley-Davidson 1000cc for it (in much better condition) in order to stop what I considered to be an important machine from leaving the country.'

1929 Harley-Davidson 29 'J' twin cylinder

988cc (61 cubic inch)

Side exhaust, overhead inlet valves

Tyres: 28 X 3 beaded edge

Forks: standard Harley-Davidson

Cast-iron flywheels

Cast-iron pistons

Mushroom tappets

Harley-Davidson generator and electrics

Carburettor: Schebler deluxe

3-speed transmission

Steve Scurr

I didn't know anything about the value of Harleys

'**When I purchased my Harley Roadster** I had in mind the phrase "It is easier to ask for forgiveness than to ask for permission". The transaction landed me with sixteen months of marital stress that could well have been avoided with a little more thought and logic. Let me first say that, prior to all this, I had not owned — or even thought about owning — a bike for over twenty-six years. I am a builder by trade and I was asked by a good friend to whip up a post and rail fence around his new swimming pool. We completed the job in professional style and the following day, Ian, the owner of the new fence, suggested a bottle of his father's home-brew would be in order.

'We were well into the second bottle when Ian mentioned that he needed to sell his Harley. Using terms I did not understand he indicated that he had signed up for another, bigger model. I am renowned for being a spendthrift and so, true to form, I immediately said, "I'll take it!" I didn't know anything about the value of Harleys, but the price sounded fair and so, off I went, into the worst scam of my life.

'Ian was very pleased and it wasn't until we were well into the third bottle that he ventured to ask what I thought Laurie, my wife, would say about all this. "No problem," I replied, "We just won't tell her." Now I have to say that it was at this point that the fun started going out of the sale for Ian. However, we agreed that only three of us would know. He had to tell his wife that the bike was sold, so that he could proceed with his new purchase.

'All went well for about five months until, at a function, my wife said to Ian's wife: "I understand your birthday present was another bloody Harley." In front of everyone I said, "I'll tell Laurie tonight when we get home." The strain of keeping it a secret was becoming too much for all concerned.

'However, since there had already been a few untruths pasted, I decided I might as well be hung for a sheep as for a lamb, and so I asked a couple of friends if they wanted to have shares in a bike. They agreed, but only after I told them it would cost them a dollar each and that for their money they would get just one quick ride. With this in hand I fronted up to my wife with the news that I had bought a Harley, but with two other partners. I told her it was an investment.

'Two months later the gearbox blew and I — and only I — was faced with a bill of some thirty-six-hundred dollars and, suddenly, an absence of partners to assist with repairs. It's amazing how disloyal your friends can be. So, after several months of living in rented garages, the beast now lives at home, not a popular addition, but here to stay.

'Maybe it is the midlife thing, but the "new toy syndrome" has not passed and, given the volume of stress I put myself under on a weekly basis, I find the occasional thirty-minute blast is an absolute must for my own well-being. By the way, I'm still married and I have two beautiful children who think Harleys are OK.'

1982 Harley-Davidson Roadster

Paul Gallagher

For some strange reason lawyers are not supposed to ride motorcycles

As a lawyer on Auckland's North Shore, Paul Gallagher feels his passion for motorcycling does not fit easily with his professional image. Maybe that's part of the attraction.

'I have been riding motorcycles since I was sixteen. As a teenager, I was absolutely determined to get my own wheels. I simply kept on at my father until one day, in desperation, he suggested that if I had to become mobile, then why didn't I consider buying a scooter or something. Well, that was my opportunity — but there was no way I was going to be seen dead riding a scooter, so he agreed to allow me to buy a "little" motorbike. In no time flat I was the proud owner of a 250cc Suzuki. I taught myself to ride on deserted country roads, became thoroughly hooked and have remained so ever since.

'I have owned all sorts of bikes over the years but my preference has tended to be for big fast sports tourers, which can acquit themselves reasonably well in a wide range of situations. I prefer to cover long distances when time allows and I find that getting out on the highway gets the adrenalin pumping and helps put my life back in perspective. Works every time for me.

'My occupation surprises some people: for some strange reason, lawyers are not supposed to ride motorcycles. Well, I have only one word to say to that — bollocks! I was riding bikes well before I had even thought of becoming a lawyer and, therefore, I guess I should be regarded as a biker who became a lawyer, rather than a lawyer who became a biker. I can go for a long hard ride somewhere and return absolutely dog tired, but the one thing that is always there is a smile from ear to ear. I can cope with things so much better when I have been for a ride.

'I have been riding for twenty-eight years now, and bikes have gotten very much faster, much more reliable and generally safer and easier to ride. What hasn't changed for the better is the attitude of many car drivers and their approach to bikes and their riders. They still try to out-accelerate us, cut us off and generally do stupid, life-threatening things.

'My wife, who would probably describe herself at times as a "biker widow", does not share my motorcycling vice. That suits me fine — you can travel faster without a pillion passenger. The standing joke in our family is that motorcycles come first and second, then comes wife, family, business etcetera. Only a fellow motorcyclist will understand that it couldn't be any other way.'

1999 Honda VTR 1000 FX

Engine: liquid-cooled 4-stroke, V-twin

DOHC 8-valve

Compression ratio: 9.4:1

Power: 81 kw (standard)

Torque: 97 Nm at 7500 rpm

Starter: electric

Transmission: 6-speed

Wheelbase: 1430 mm

Seat height: 810 mm

Ground clearance: 135 mm

Dry weight: 192 kg

Modifications: two Brothers Racing headers and pipes; Dynojet Carb kit; front forks re-valved with stiffer springs; Ohlins rear shock; aftermarket fairing screen; Scott Oiler

Len Perry

I rode my first bike in 1927, when I was fifteen

The legendary L.V. Perry decided finally to hang up his helmet last year, at the age of 87. This photograph, taken at his home in Auckland, shows Len in front of his wall of trophies.

To many New Zealand motorcycle enthusiasts, Len Perry is already the stuff of legend. He began his long racing career in 1928 and during the following 71 years managed to win no less than 42 New Zealand national titles. Len also represented New Zealand at the Isle of Man TT races, won eight New Zealand TT titles at Waiheke Island, won the New Zealand Grass-Track title and the New Zealand solo title for speedway riding — the list of his achievements makes impressive reading. Where did it all start?

'My dad was a farmer and I rode my first bike in 1927, when I was fifteen. I rode my first race at Henning's Speedway in Mangere in 1928 on a B4 AJS. I won, too! There was I on a B4 when other riders were competing on much better machinery. I was an inexperienced novice and I could hardly believe that I'd won. After the B4 I rode a KTT Velocette, the first one to arrive in New Zealand. I won eighteen New Zealand titles on that machine.

'In 1932, I got together with Henry Fletcher and we laid the first New Zealand TT course at Waiheke Island. It was a hard course, a hundred and sixty-eight miles long over gravel roads. The TT ran at Waiheke until 1950, when it moved to Seagrove Aerodrome.'

Len went on to represent New Zealand at the Isle of Man TT races, but his memories of that particular venue are not all wonderful. In 1939, during a practice lap, Len crashed his Velocette KTT and lost a finger as a result.

Then came the war and Len became Sergeant Perry of the RNZAF. He served in New Zealand and the Pacific, and almost lost his life when, during a test flight in a Catalina off the Fijian coast, the aircraft stalled and plummeted 5000 feet into the ocean. From a crew of seventeen, only five survived and they had to spend a gruelling 24 hours in a rubber dinghy before being rescued.

After the war, Len's life was no less dangerous. He won the majority of his racing trophies in these post-war years, including seven of his eight TT titles. Len was interested in every aspect of motorcycling and it was during these years also that he pursued his ambitions in speedway, winning the New Zealand solo title. He even tried his skill at riding on three wheels and he came out on top again, winning the Auckland sidecar title. Later years saw Len notching up other successes on a Vincent 1000cc bike.

In 1951 Len went to the Isle of Man again, this time to represent New Zealand on a Norton. The three members of the New Zealand team won three titles between them, thus putting New Zealand on the map when it came to road racing.

Len's memories of his golden years in motorcycling go back a long way. In 1954 he rode his last grass-track race at the Avondale Racecourse. Len regards grass-track racing as a challenging sport.

'It was extremely difficult. The grass was slippery, the ground rough and hard and the races were long. You must remember that the bikes weren't as sophisticated then as they are nowadays. TT racing, too, has changed since the early days. We raced over a hundred miles in one race and all on gravel. It was a challenge to build a machine that could take it and another challenge to ride it. I remember when Leo Simpson was hit on the nose during the New Zealand Grand Prix. His goggles filled with blood and he couldn't see. He stopped, changed his goggles and blocked his nose with cotton wool. I believe he was following me at the time.'

Having only just retired it will be interesting to see if Len really can manage to leave his leathers in the wardrobe.

Val & Paul Davis

Paul, a professional photographer, and Val, then a schoolteacher, met and married in 1979. Both English, they and their two children emigrated to New Zealand in 1992. Exactly one year later they returned to Britain, only to re-emigrate to New Zealand in 1995.

Val and Paul now run their photographic and marketing services business from their purpose-built studio in Coatesville, north of Auckland. The studio is also used for charity cabaret evenings, with Val and Paul joining talented young musicians and singers from all over Auckland. Paul comperes the shows, while Val performs her own brand of humerous poetry.

Two of the photographs in this book were submitted to the prestigious annual Kodak Awards competition for professional photographers. Both won awards, one a gold and one a silver.